10 Performance-Based Projects

Grades
3–5

10 Performance-Based Projects for the Language Arts Classroom

Todd Stanley

PRUFROCK PRESS INC.
WACO, TEXAS

Edited by Katy McDowall

Cover design by Raquel Trevino and layout design by Allegra Denbo

ISBN-13: 978-1-61821-578-9

Printed in the United States of America.

Prufrock Press Inc.
P.O. Box 8813
Waco, TX 76714-8813
Phone: (800) 998-2208
Fax: (800) 240-0333
http://www.prufrock.com

TABLE OF CONTENTS

INTRODUCTION

Why Project-Based Learning?

Twenty-first century skills, or survival skills, as termed by Tony Wagner in his book *The Global Achievement Gap* (2014), involve students being able to do more than memorize facts and instead apply skills and, more importantly, problem solve (Stoof, Martens, Van Merriënboer, & Bastiaens, 2002). In short, teachers are tasked with the difficult job of trying to create thinkers. This results from businesses complaining that the best and brightest students that the educational system is sending their way are very intelligent but woefully inept at figuring out problems, arguing students know a lot of "facts" but are not "competent" (Bastiaens & Martens, 2000). Any teacher able to help students become these thinkers would be providing them with an advantage when they enter the real world.

The educational system has to do a better job of preparing students to solve real-world problems. How do we do that in the current system of standards and testing? With so much at stake on these achievement tests, the bigger question is: How often in life are we asked to take a pencil-and-paper test? Not very often unless you count online personality quizzes. In real life we are usually dealing with projects, either at work, home, or other settings. If we truly want to get students ready for the real world, we should be teaching them how to handle the real-world dilemma of a project.

As mentioned in *Project-Based Learning for Gifted Students: A Handbook for the 21st-Century Classroom* (Stanley, 2012), according to the Buck Institute for Education, research studies have demonstrated project-based learning can:

- increase academic achievement on standardized assessment tests;
- teach math, economics, social studies, science, medical skills, and health-related subjects more effectively than traditional teaching methods;
- increase long-term retention of knowledge, skill development, and student and teacher satisfaction;
- prepare students to integrate and explain concepts better than traditional instructional methods;
- prove especially helpful for low-achieving students;
- present a workable model for larger school reform; and
- help students to master 21st-century skills such as communication, independent and critical thinking, and research. (p. 4)

This is why project-based learning is such a good fit for creating such thinkers. It has been discovered that students:

- prefer to structure their own tasks they are working on and establish deadlines as opposed to having the teacher assign them (Dunn, Dunn, & Price, 1984; Renzulli, Smith, & Reis, 1982; Stewart, 1981);
- learn more and retain content more accurately when allowed to work on projects in which they set the pace (Whitener, 1989);
- show an increased benefit in learning when they teach each other through projects (Johnsen-Harrris, 1983; Kingsley, 1986);
- show improvement in cooperative learning skills when working in groups because they must work together to solve problems (Peterson, 1997); and
- show increased engagement after participating in PBL than students who did not (Grant & Branch, 2005; Horton, Hedetniemi, Weigert, & Wagner, 2006; Johnston, 2004; Jones & Kalinowski, 2007; Ljung & Blackwell, 1996; McMiller, Lee, Saroop, Green, & Johnson, 2006; Toolin, 2004).

Based on this research, a better question to ask is not why use project-based learning, but rather why not use project-based learning?

What Are the Advantages of Using PBL in a Language Arts Classroom?

Project-based learning is an excellent vehicle to teach 21st-century skills. In *21st Century Skills: Learning for Life in Our Times* (2009), Bernie Trilling and Charles Fadel mentioned, among valuable 21st-century skills, eight specific skills that PBL can effectively teach:

1. public speaking,
2. problem solving,
3. collaboration,
4. critical thinking,
5. information literacy,
6. creativity,
7. adaptability, and
8. self-direction. (p. viii)

Many of these are crucial for the language classroom. These are skills that can be worked into many PBL projects and that allow students to develop confidence in them over time. They also tie in to many Common Core State Standards for English Language Arts (CCSS-ELA) for grades 3–5, such as:

- Reading Informational Text:
  - RI.3.4, 4.4, 5.4: Determine the meaning of general academic and domain-specific words or phrases in a text relevant to a *grade 3–5 topic or subject area.*
  - RI.3.5: Use text features and search tools (e.g., key words, sidebars, hyperlinks) to locate information relevant to a given topic efficiently.
  - RI.3.7: Draw on information from multiple print or digital sources, demonstrating the ability to locate an answer to a question quickly or to solve a problem efficiently.
  - RI.3.4: Integrate information from two texts on the same topic in order to write or speak about the subject knowledgeably.

- Writing:
  - W.3.7, 4.7, 5.7: Conduct short research projects that build knowledge through investigation of different aspects of a topic.

  - W.4.8: Recall relevant information from experiences or gather relevant information from print and digital sources; take notes and categorize information, and provide a list of sources.
  - W.4.9, 5.9: Draw evidence from literary or informational texts to support analysis, reflection, and research.

- Speaking and Listening:
  - SL.3.6: Speak in complete sentences when appropriate to task and situation in order to provide requested detail or clarification.
  - SL.4.4: Report on a topic or text, tell a story, or recount an experience in an organized manner, using appropriate facts and relevant, descriptive details to support main ideas or themes; speak clearly at an understandable pace.
  - SL.4.5: Add audio recordings and visual displays to presentations when appropriate to enhance the development of main ideas or themes.
  - SL.5.2: Summarize the points a speaker makes and explain how each claim is supported by reasons and evidence.

- Language:
  - L.4.1: Demonstrate command of the conventions of standard English grammar and usage when writing or speaking.
  - L.4.3: Use knowledge of language and its conventions when writing, speaking, reading, or listening.

Trilling and Fadel (2009) define information literacy as the ability to:

- access information efficiently and effectively,
- evaluate information critically and competently, and
- use information accurately and creatively. (p. 65)

This is not only a skill for the classroom—this is a skill for life. If you want to figure out what time to see a movie or where you need to go for your appointment at a new dentist, you will have to figure out where to get this information, how to tell if the information is correct, and how to use the information. Any time you are doing research in the classroom, information literacy will be very valuable. This information can come in the form of print resources or electronic resources.

Project-based learning allows students to use information literacy to complete a given project. Research papers, presentations, portfolios, and debates are just a few types of performance-based assessments that require information literacy. Like many others, this is a skill that must be taught purposefully. If we as teachers do not lay the foundation, students will develop their own habits, many of them unproductive. Trying to break a student of a bad habit while teaching her a new one is much more difficult than simply making sure she is applying a skill correctly while learning it for the first time. One mistake we often make as teachers is assuming that students already know how to do something, especially when it comes to Internet research. Depending on what grade we teach, we might assume this has already been taught or that students have been surfing the Internet for years. Making sure students have an understanding of how to properly research both print and electronic resources is not something you should take for granted.

In the end, the more experience students get with information literacy, the better they are going to become at it. As the teacher, you need to make sure this exposure is guided so that their experiences develop good practices rather than bad habits. Performance-based assessment will allow you to do this.

Public speaking is an invaluable skill for any person to have. One of the major reasons for this is that not everyone is able to do it. If you are someone who can speak in public and do it well, you have an advantage over others. This fear of public speaking can be overcome, especially if you start the process before it becomes a deep-rooted fear. Experience tends to be the best coping mechanism. The more experience someone has at something, the less likely she is going to panic.

You need to give your students the chance to gain experience without the fear of getting hurt. In short, you have to provide opportunities for your students to speak in class. Every experience you give them will provide that much more confidence in their ability to publicly speak. Your classroom needs to feel like a place where mistakes can be made and where students do not have to be perfect. Mistakes are how some of the best lessons are learned.

There are several reasons why the ability to publicly speak is so important, but here are a few:

- Public speaking increases self-confidence.
- Public speaking makes you more comfortable around other people.

- Public speaking is one of the most effective ways to get your message across.
- Skills learned through public speaking can boost performance in other areas in life.
- Public speaking allows you to demonstrate your knowledge.
- Public speaking allows you to improve upon your knowledge.
- Public speaking differentiates you in the workplace.
- Public speaking prepares you to be a leader. (Ryan, 2013, para. 5)

When students get out in the real world and are looking for a job, they will likely be competing with thousands of other graduates. What will make someone stand out from all of these people? What will allow potential employers to notice him over the others? The ability to effectively speak in public is an obvious answer.

Using PBL in your classroom will give your students the experience to become more comfortable with public speaking. The more confidence they gain, the better they are going to be at it. The skills of collaboration, self-direction, and adaptability would come naturally with any PBL no matter what the topic, as long as the teacher is having students work in groups and allowing them the space to develop independence.

What Sorts of Products Could Be Used in a Language Arts Classroom?

As laid out in *Performance-Based Assessment for 21st-Century Skills* (Stanley, 2014), there are 10 different types of assessments that can be used in a project-based learning environment:

1. oral presentations,
2. debates/speeches,
3. role playing,
4. group discussions,
5. interviews,
6. portfolios,
7. exhibitions,
8. essays,

9. research papers, and
10. journals/student logs. (p. 43)

There are, of course, many other types, but these are the 10 this book will be focusing on and providing examples of.

Keep in mind these project plans can be changed, added to, rearranged, and anything else you need to do to make them effective for your students. There are some that contain lessons that could be used for other projects. For example, many of the plans call for students to conduct research, but Project 8, the research paper, has a mini-lesson on how students can conduct research. This lesson could be applied to many of the projects, so move aspects around and set it up the way that works best for your students.

1 Oral Presentation

Much of what a student knows can be expressed in an oral presentation. Classrooms are full of the type of student who raises his hand and can provide insightful, meaningful responses when taking part in discussion, but as soon as you ask that same student to write down his thoughts, you are lucky to get a one- or two-word written response. He is not able, or more likely, not willing, to give you the same insightful responses in writing. In dealing with these kinds of students, the question for me became: Why couldn't this student provide his answers orally, especially if it meant getting responses like he did in class? On the flip side are those students who do not know how to express themselves in an oral presentation, and the acquisition of the skill is very valuable to them.

What It Looks Like

Oral presentations can take several forms, but they typically consist of an informative speech designed to educate an audience. Some of the forms can be:

- an individual or group report,
- an oral briefing,
- an oral exam,
- a panel discussion, or
- an oral critique.

The student's goal in an oral presentation is to verbally teach classmates or the audience what she has learned after researching a particular topic or skill. A successful oral presentation needs to be set up just like an essay would, with a topic sentence, supporting details, and several drafts before the final presentation. This structure is something that should be taught to students. This can be done with modeling, looking at exemplary examples of great oral presentations, or practicing presentations with no consequences.

Recommended Reading Talk

Do you have a favorite book or a book that you really enjoyed recently? How would you convince others to read this book? How would you tell your friends about this book?

In this project, students will give a 10-minute oral presentation about one of their favorite books or a book they have read recently and enjoyed. The purpose of the presentation is to convince others to read the book by showing what they liked about it.

Connections to CCSS

- RL.3.1
- RL.4.1
- RL.5.1
- SL.3.4
- SL.4.4
- SL.5.4

Materials

- Project Outline: Recommended Reading Talk (student copies)
- Suggested Timeline
- Lesson: How to Give a Recommended Reading Talk
- Lesson: What Makes a Good Presentation?
- Handout 1.1: Discussion Questions (student copies)
- Handout 1.2: What Makes a Good Presentation? (student copies)
- Handout 1.3: Peer Review (student copies)
- Product Rubric (student copies)

Name: ______________________________ Date: ______________

PROJECT OUTLINE

Recommended Reading Talk

Directions: Do you have a favorite book or a book that you really enjoyed recently? How would you convince others to read this book? How would you tell your friends about this book?

You will give a 10-minute oral presentation about one of your favorite books or a book you have read recently and enjoyed. The purpose of the presentation is to convince others to read the book by showing what you liked about it.

SUGGESTED TIMELINE

DAY				
1 Introduce the project with Lesson: How to Give a Recommended Reading Talk.	**2** Have students bring in the book they would like to review.	**3** Have students answer questions about their book on Handout 1.1: Discussion Questions.	**4** Have students continue to answer the questions on Handout 1.1.	**5** Have students finish answering the questions on Handout 1.1.
6 Conduct Lesson: What Makes a Good Presentation? and distribute Handout 1.2.	**7** Have students practice their presentations.	**8** Have students practice their presentations.	**9** Have students conduct peer reviews (see Handout 1.3).	**10** Begin student presentations (see Product Rubric).
11 Continue student presentations.	**12** Continue student presentations.	**13** Continue student presentations.	**14** Continue student presentations.	**15** Continue student presentations.

LESSON

How to Give a Recommended Reading Talk

Distribute Handout 1.1: Discussion Questions. Model a recommended reading talk for students by answering the questions for a book that you enjoy. The following sample responses use *A Mutiny in Time* (Infinity Ring #1) by James Dashner.

1. Give a brief overview of what the book is about. Imagine you are writing the back cover of the book for the publisher and you need to convince someone picking it up in the store to read the book. What parts of the story would you share to get him or her to do that? What parts would you leave out so that you do not ruin the book for him or her?

The story is about two fifth-grade kids, Dak and Sera, who discover that their parents are part of a secret society known as the Hystorians. There is another group called the SQ that runs the government and is very powerful. SQ is trying to imprison or stop the members of the Hystorians from fixing what are called "breaks." Breaks are points in time where someone has gone back and tampered with history.

When the SQ attacks the Hystorian headquarters, Dak, Sera, and a young Hystorian named Riq use a device called the Infinity Ring to escape back in time. The Infinity Ring is programmed to take them to points in time that the SQ tampered with. The three youngsters must put history right so that things can go back to the way they were. They make a first stop during the American Revolution where Dak's parents are captured and then escape to right before Columbus sailed his expedition to the New World. They have to find where the break is while trying not to get captured by members of the SQ called Time Wardens.

2. Pretend you are a book reviewer working for the newspaper. They've asked you to write a review of the book for their readers. What is your opinion of the book and characters? What type of person/reader would enjoy reading this book? Be sure to support your opinions with proof from the story.

I really enjoyed this book because of the time travel. I love history and so getting to read about them traveling to meet famous historical figures and interacting with people from hundreds of years ago is interesting to me. I was especially excited when they went back to the American Revolution because it is one of my favorite times in history, but I was disappointed that they did not stay very long. And with there being a secret society, it reminds me of series such as The 39 Clues and Harry Potter, which I really enjoyed.

I like the main characters, Dak and Sera. They have a very strong friendship, which is rare between a girl and a boy without some sort of romantic connection. They are more like brother and sister. There is a character called Riq, who I do not care for because he and Dak are constantly arguing with one another and trying to show one another up.

Anyone who likes adventure books will enjoy this book. The action is constant in the book and sometimes it feels as though there is not even a chance to catch your breath. Once you finish you're given another adventure that you can play online. This map shows where the next place to go is so you can continue the adventure. This is also the first part in a six-book series so you know the story is going to continue for a while longer.

3. Which character in the book is the most like you? Tell us who that character is and why he or she is similar to you. Give examples from the story to explain why you think that character is similar to you. Think about:
   - his or her personality,
   - his or her hobbies,
   - how he or she feels about different things, and
   - his or her family.

I would say the person who is most like me is Dak. Dak is sort of a know-it-all and sometimes I can certainly act like that. He is cocky, especially when it comes to his rivalry with Riq. He also is obsessed with history, which is a hobby of mine as well. Dak also tends to be a little impulsive, acting before he thinks in many occasions. When I was younger I tended to do that too much and it ended up getting me into trouble, as it does with Dak.

There are a couple of differences though. Dak loses his parents when they are transported to the American Revolution, and although he seems upset at first, it doesn't last very long. I think I would be much more upset if that happened to me.

4. After reading the whole book, tell us if you would want to be a character in this story, or not. Make sure you describe at least three events from the story and tell us why those events would either make you want to, or not want to be part of this story. Think about these things:
   - Were the characters people you would want to be around?
   - Were the events in the story events that you would want to be involved in?
   - Was it a time period that you would like to live in?

Although Dak is like me, I don't know that I would like to be him. The task Dak and Sera have been given is a lot of pressure, especially for a young kid. (1) The SQuare device requires them to solve riddles in order to get clues, but just one mistake and it will explode. I am not sure I would like being under that much pressure. (2) Dak loses his parents and that is not something I would want to do.

Also, although I love history, I am not quite sure I would want to go back in time to these places. There is a lot of danger there—even if a group such as the SQ isn't trying to hunt you down. (3) When they go back to the American Revolution soldiers are pointing guns at them and threatening to shoot them. That would be very scary.

5. If you could change one thing about this book, what would it be and why? First, explain the part in detail. Then describe why you would want to change the part. Finally, show what you would do differently. Or, if you enjoyed the book and don't want to change anything, which part of the book would you like to expand? Maybe you want to know more about a relationship between two characters or more about a scene. Make sure you include why you want to know more.

*If I could change anything with the book, it would be to give it one central bad guy. Right now the antagonist of the book is the SQ but there is no central figure like a Voldemort or a Sauron (*The Hobbit*). Because it is a faceless society who they are against, there is no bad guy to focus in on as the central antagonist. I think it would make the book stronger if there were someone like that.*

I would have expanded the part when they went back to the American Revolution. They are only there for about 5 minutes and then they are whisked away to the time of Christopher Columbus. I would want this expanded because I got excited when they popped up in the Revolutionary times and was hoping for more. I would also like to know what happened to Dak's parents after they were captured by the British.

6. If you were to write a sequel to the book, what would it be about? Why would you choose that particular storyline? Would you bring back all of the characters? Why or why not?

If I could write a sequel to this book I would have them go to the ancient Mayan civilization. This is a fascinating time period, as the empire, which existed for hundreds of years, suddenly ceased to exist. There is so much not known about them. It would be interesting to see what the author comes up with to answer these questions.

Luckily I do not have to imagine this too much because it turns out that Dak and Sera go to Mayan society in the fourth book.

Although I am sure Riq will end up being an important character because he knows so many languages, I wish they would get rid of him and just focus on the relationship between Dak and Sera. I like their friendship and sometimes having the third character there just gets in the way of that.

7. If you could write this book from another character's point of view, who would you choose? Why? How would this change the story and why?

The book goes back and forth from Daq to Sera's perspective. Although I do not care for the character, it would be interesting to see the story from the perspective of Riq. I think he is portrayed as not likeable because you mostly see him from the eyes of Dak. If the story were told from the perspective of Riq then I am sure Dak would be the character who is difficult to like.

It might also be interesting to hear Dak's parents' story when they get captured during the American Revolution. So far in the second and third book, we do not know what has happened to them and it would be good to know if they were able to escape.

LESSON

What Makes a Good Presentation?

There are certain elements that make up a good oral presentation. Distribute Handout 1.2: What Makes a Good Presentation? and review the 10 things for students to consider:

1. Keep consistent eye contact.
2. Use a strong, confident voice.
3. Avoid "umms," "ahhhs," and "likes."
4. Keep your hands in the correct place. (Don't put them in your pockets or cross your arms.)
5. Don't read your information. Present it.
6. Show you care about your topic. (Don't use a monotone voice.)
7. Stand up straight.
8. Be prepared. (Practice ahead of time.)
9. Maintain professionalism. (Don't giggle or say inappropriate things.)
10. Have a flow to your presentation. (Have notes to fall back on if you get stuck.)

Have students watch an example of a good oral presentation. Good examples include:

- TED Talks
- Dr. Martin Luther King Jr's "I Have a Dream Speech"
- Infomercials
- John Green Nerdfighters Presentations
- Book talks on YouTube

Have students listen and go through the list on Handout 1.2, identifying whether or not the presenter met all of the requirements of a good presentation.

Name: ______________________________ Date: ______________

HANDOUT 1.1

Discussion Questions

Directions: Use these discussion questions to guide your book talk. Remember to answer them with lots of detail and cite text examples to back up your point whenever you can.

1. **Give a brief overview of what the book is about.** Imagine you are writing the back cover of the book for the publisher and you need to convince someone picking it up in the store to read this book. What parts of the story would you share to get him or her to do that? What parts would you leave out so that you do not ruin the book for him or her?

2. **Pretend you are a book reviewer working for the newspaper.** They've asked you to write a review of the book. What is your opinion of the book and characters? What type of person would enjoy reading this book? Be sure to support your opinions with proof from the story.

3. **Which character in the book is the most like you?** Tell us who that character is and why he or she is similar to you. Give examples from the story to explain why you think that character is similar to you. Think about:
   - his or her personality,
   - his or her hobbies,
   - how he or she feels about different things, and
   - his or her family.

Name: ______________________________ Date: ______________

Handout 1.1: Discussion Questions, *continued*

4. **After reading the book, tell us if you would want to be a character in this story or not.** Make sure you describe at least three events from the story and why those events would either make you want or not want to be part of this story. Think about these things:
   - Were the characters people you would want to be around?
   - Were the events in the story events that you would want to be involved in?
   - Was it a time period that you would like to live in?

5. **If you could change one thing about this book, what would it be and why?** First, explain the part in detail. Then describe why you would want to change the part. Finally, show what you would do differently. Or, if you enjoyed the book and don't want to change anything, which part of the book would you like to expand? Maybe you want to know more about a relationship between two characters or more about a scene. Make sure you include why you want to know more.

6. **If you were to write a sequel to the book, what would it be about?** Why would you choose that particular storyline? Would you bring back all of the characters? Why or why not?

7. **If you could write this book from another character's point of view, who would you choose?** Why? How would this change the story and why?

Name: ______________________________ Date: ______________

HANDOUT 1.2

What Makes a Good Presentation?

Directions: There are certain elements that make up a good oral presentation. Here are 10 things to consider:

1. Keep consistent eye contact.
2. Use a strong, confident voice.
3. Avoid "umms," "ahhhs," and "likes."
4. Keep your hands in the correct place. (Don't put them in your pockets or cross your arms.)
5. Don't read your information. Present it.
6. Show you care about your topic. (Don't use a monotone voice.)
7. Stand up straight.
8. Be prepared. (Practice ahead of time.)
9. Maintain professionalism. (Don't giggle or say inappropriate things.)
10. Have a flow to your presentation. (Have notes to fall back on if you get stuck.)

Name: ______________________________ Date: ______________

HANDOUT 1.3

Peer Review

Directions: Circle whether your peer did or did not do each of the following.

Peer's Name: ______________________ Book: ____________________

1.	He or she kept consistent eye contact.	Yes	No
2.	He or she used a strong, confident voice.	Yes	No
3.	He or she did not use "umms," "ahhhs," and "likes."	Yes	No
4.	He or she used his or her hands correctly (not in his or her pockets or arms crossed).	Yes	No
5.	He or she presented his or her information; he or she did not read it.	Yes	No
6.	He or she cares about his or her topic (no monotone voice).	Yes	No
7.	He or she stood up straight.	Yes	No
8.	He or she was prepared (practiced ahead of time).	Yes	No
9.	He or she maintained professionalism (no giggling or saying inappropriate things).	Yes	No
10.	His or her presentation flowed (and he or she had notes to fall back on if he or she get stuck).	Yes	No

Name: ________________________ Date: ______________

PRODUCT RUBRIC

Recommended Reading

Overall	Presentation	Structure	Content
Excellent (A)	◆ Presenter spoke clearly and slowly and could be heard the entire time. ◆ Presenter's demeanor was professional, and it sounded as though he or she rehearsed several times. ◆ Presentation was organized in a manner that made it easy to follow and understand.	◆ Presenter spoke for close to 10 minutes. ◆ Presenter followed the outline of the presentation, answering all of the questions with great detail and citing examples.	◆ Presenter referred to details and examples in the text when explaining what the text said explicitly. ◆ Presenter referred to details and examples in the text when drawing inferences from the text.
Good (B–C)	◆ Presenter spoke clearly and slowly but was difficult to hear once or twice. ◆ Presenter's demeanor was professional throughout much of the presentation but lacked at times, and it sounded like he or she rehearsed but could have used more practice. ◆ Presentation was organized in a manner that made it easy to follow and understand, but there were a couple of instances where it was difficult to follow.	◆ Presenter spoke for 7–9 minutes. ◆ Presenter followed the outline of the presentation, answering all of the questions, but could have more detail and examples.	◆ Presenter referred to details and examples in the text when explaining what the text said explicitly, but sometimes the explanations were not clear. ◆ Presenter referred to details and examples in the text when drawing inferences from the text most of the time but did not consistently provide specific details from the book.
Needs Improvement (D–F)	◆ Presenter could not be heard for a good portion and/or did not speak slowly and clearly. ◆ Presenter's demeanor was not professional throughout much of the presentation, causing a distraction, and it did not sound as though he or she rehearsed. ◆ Presentation was not very organized, making it difficult to follow and understand.	◆ Presenter spoke for 6 minutes or less. ◆ Presenter did not follow the outline of the presentation and did not answer all of the questions.	◆ Presenter did not refer to details and examples in the text when explaining what the text says explicitly. ◆ Presenter did not refer to details and examples in the text when drawing inferences from the text.

2 Debate/ Speech

This is another form of oral presentation, but instead of seeking to inform, the main goal is to persuade. Debates and speeches are a higher level of thinking because they don't just convey information but employ tactics to convince someone that one student's opinions or viewpoints are more valuable than another's. It is a process more complicated than the usual presentation because it looks at "ethos, the credibility of the speaker; logos, the logical proof and reasoning presented in the words of the speech; and pathos, the use of emotional appeals to influence the audience" (Brydon & Scott, 2000).

What It Looks Like

Debates are especially great to use when the concept being taught is ambiguous or allows for multiple perspectives. Speeches are another form of this persuasive oral presentation. While delivering a speech, the student is either playing a role or representing a organization. He must convince people of his platform or ideals. Although not as interactive as a debate, the speech still requires the student to tap into higher levels of thinking and make a sound argument.

Create Your Own Political Party

In this project, students will be divided into groups of three and create their own political party. Like all political parties, they need to develop a platform that displays their beliefs as a party. This platform will eventually be displayed in presidential and vice-presidential speeches and a campaign poster at an upcoming caucus.

Connections to CCSS

- W.3.1
- W.4.1
- W.5.1
- SL.3.4
- SL.3.5
- SL.3.6
- SL.4.4
- SL.4.5
- SL.4.6
- SL.5.4
- SL.5.5
- SL.5.6

Materials

- Project Outline: Create Your Own Political Party (student copies)
- Suggested Timeline
- Lesson: How to Write a Good Speech
- Lesson: How to Give a Good Speech
- Handout 2.1: Political Party Graphic Organizer (student copies)
- Handout 2.2: Basic Structure of Your Political Speech (student copies)
- Handout 2.3: How to Give a Good Speech (student copies)
- Handout 2.4: Peer Review (student copies)
- Product Rubric (student copies)

Name: ______________________________ Date: ______________

PROJECT OUTLINE

Create Your Own Political Party

Directions: You and your group will create your own political party. Like all political parties, you need to develop a platform that displays your beliefs as a party. This platform will eventually be displayed in presidential and vice-presidential speeches and a campaign poster at an upcoming caucus.

Members of your group of three will take on the following roles:

- **Presidential Candidate:** This person will be the primary candidate and will have to give a speech at the caucus.
- **Vice-Presidential Candidate:** This person will act as the running mate and will have to give a speech at the caucus.
- **Campaign Manager:** This person will be in charge of the campaign, helping to write the speeches and create the campaign poster.

You must decide on the issues your party will support and where it stands. Choose six of the following:

- Taxes
- Foreign Affairs
- Environment
- Defense Spending
- Health Care
- Social Security/Unemployment
- Education
- Civil Rights
- Immigration
- Economy

Each candidate, with the help of the campaign manager, will write a speech he or she will present at the caucus. The speeches should convey the major parts of the party's platform. Each candidate must cover three of the party's issues (i.e., the president will address three and vice president a different three). The speeches will be evaluated mostly on content but also on presentation, so choose candidates you feel are good speakers.

Your political party must also create a campaign poster that includes a slogan, a party mascot, the candidates' names, and the party name.

SUGGESTED TIMELINE

DAY 1	2	3	4	5
Introduce the project and form groups.	Have groups research/ develop their stance on issues using Handout 2.1: Political Party Graphic Organizer.	Have groups continue to work on Handout 2.1.	Have groups continue to work on Handout 2.1.	Have groups complete Handout 2.1 and be ready to write their speeches.
6	**7**	**8**	**9**	**10**
Conduct Lesson: How to Write a Good Speech and distribute Handout 2.2.	Have groups write their speeches and create campaign posters.	Have groups write their speeches and create campaign posters.	Have groups write their speeches and create campaign posters.	Have groups write their speeches and create campaign posters.
11	**12**	**13**		
Conduct Lesson: What Makes a Good Speech? and distribute Handout 2.3.	Have students practice their speeches.	Have students present and conduct peer reviews (see Handout 2.4 and Product Rubric).		

LESSON

How to Write a Good Speech

Show students tutorials on how to write a good speech. Recommended online tutorials include:

- "How to Write a Campaign Speech" by Laura Minnigerode (https://www.youtube.com/watch?v=_q7DM8WkzAQ)
- "How to Start Your Speech (3 excellent openings)" by Jeff Roy (https://www.youtube.com/watch?v=tCBZQ8Jvg9k)

Hold a discussion afterward about common elements, such as the pace, the volume, the clarity of ideas, and the body language of the speaker. These can be turned into suggestions that students can use in their own speeches. Distribute Handout 2.2: Basic Structure of a Political Speech for students to review.

LESSON

What Makes a Good Speech?

Have students look at actual speeches to make sure they follow the basic structure of political speeches and how well the speaker delivers the speech.

Examples of campaign or political speeches that students can view online include:

- William Jennings Bryan's "Cross of Gold" speech
- Ronald Reagan's "Tear Down this Wall" speech
- John F. Kennedy's "Ask Not What Your Country Can Do For You" speech

Distribute Handout 2.3: How to Give a Good Speech. Have students read one of the most famous speeches, Abraham Lincoln's Gettysburg Address. Discuss the speech with students. Have them analyze the speech and how well Lincoln followed these tips:

1. Make your points short and clear.

2. Be professional.

3. Speak with confidence, authority.

4. Try to make a connection.

5. Use imagery, examples.

6. End strong.

Name: ______________________________ Date: ______________

HANDOUT 2.1

Political Party Graphic Organizer

Directions: The presidential candidate needs to address three issues in his or her speech, and the vice-presidential candidate's speech needs to address an additional three issues that fall under the party's platform. Use this graphic organizer to list the six issues the speeches will address and have a discussion about the position the party is going to take.

Issue 1:
Party's Stance:
Issue 2:
Party's Stance:
Issue 3:
Party's Stance:

Name: ______________________ Date: ______________

Handout 2.1: Political Party Graphic Organizer, *continued*

Issue 4:
Party's Stance:
Issue 5:
Party's Stance:
Issue 6:
Party's Stance:

Name: ______________________________ Date: ______________

HANDOUT 2.2

Basic Structure of Your Political Speech

Directions: Use these tips and suggestions as you write your political speech.

1. **Don't ramble; get to the point.** What is the main stance your party is taking? This needs to be conveyed early and often in your speeches so that people listening know where you stand. Your main stance should be simple enough that it can be expressed in one sentence. If you try to talk about too many things, the audience will get lost and remember nothing.

2. **Write like you talk.** There is a huge difference between reading something and the spoken word. If you sound like you are reading your speech then it will come off as stilted and wooden. It should sound like more of a performance. A successful speech has a conversational tone, as though the speaker is talking directly to a person rather than a large audience.

3. **Connect with your audience.** The beginning of a speech is very important. Within the first lines, an audience decides whether you are worth listening to or not. You will want to establish a connection so the audience wants to listen to you. One way to do this is to begin you speech with a specific scenario that illustrates your main idea, such as a story. This will allow the audience to connect to you as a person rather than a politican.

4. **The main idea.** Keep things simple and make sure to tell your audience clearly your main points. You don't want them to miss these. Repetition is important but not to the point where it becomes annoying. As much as possible try to explain the why to all of your party's political stances.

5. **Seem knowledgeable.** People want candidates who know what they are talking about. One way to do this is to explain your platform issues in a manner so that you seem like you understand them. You need to explain the basic idea of the platform issue so that your audience understands it, but have lots of facts and statistics to illustrate your points. Confidence also goes a long way in making people seem like they know what they are talking about. Know the words you are speaking and pronounce them correctly.

Name: ______________________________ Date: ______________

Handout 2.1: Basic Structure of Your Political Speech, *continued*

6. **Finish strong.** Nothing is worse than spending time explaining your major points and getting the audience on your side, only to provide a weak finish and lose your audience as a result. The closing of a speech should be memorable. This could be done by using a meaningful quote, restating your party's slogan, or providing something inspirational in your own words. People should know when you have finished your speech. If they are unsure if you are done, then you have not provided a strong finish.

Note. Adapted from *Tips from the Insiders: How to Write a Political Speech* by Scholastic, n.d., retrieved from http://www.scholastic.com/teachers/article/tips-insiders-how-write-political-speech.

Name: ______________________________ Date: ______________

HANDOUT 2.3

How to Give a Good Speech

Directions: Read Abraham Lincoln's Gettysburg Address. How well does he follow the tips below?

To give a good speech, you will need to:

1. Make your points short and clear.
2. Be professional.
3. Speak with confidence, authority.
4. Try to make a connection.
5. Use imagery, examples.
6. End strong.

The Gettysburg Address

Four score and seven years ago our fathers brought forth on this continent a new nation, conceived in liberty, and dedicated to the proposition that all men are created equal.

Now we are engaged in a great civil war, testing whether that nation, or any nation so conceived and so dedicated, can long endure. We are met on a great battlefield of that war. We have come to dedicate a portion of that field, as a final resting place for those who here gave their lives that that nation might live. It is altogether fitting and proper that we should do this.

But, in a larger sense, we can not dedicate, we can not consecrate, we can not hallow this ground. The brave men, living and dead, who struggled here, have consecrated it, far above our poor power to add or detract. The world will little note, nor long remember what we say here, but it can never forget what they did here. It is for us the living, rather, to be dedicated here to the unfinished work which they who fought here have thus far so nobly advanced. It is rather for us to be here dedicated to the great task remaining before us—that from these honored dead we take increased devotion to that cause for which they gave the last full measure of devotion—that we here highly resolve that these dead shall not have died in vain—that this nation, under God, shall have a new birth of freedom—and that government of the people, by the people, for the people, shall not perish from the earth.

—Abraham Lincoln
Gettysburg, PA
November 19, 1863

Name: ______________________ Date: ______________

HANDOUT 2.4

Peer Review

Directions: Rate each of your group members on a scale of 1–10. A 10 means they did a fantastic job, contributed a lot to their part of the campaign, and it could not have been done without them. A 1 means they contributed almost nothing and actually prevented others from being able to do a good job.

Group Member's Name: ______________________

1. How would you rate this person in regards to creating the platform for your political party?

   1 2 3 4 5 6 7 8 9 10

2. How would you rate this person's contribution in the campaign process of the project?

   1 2 3 4 5 6 7 8 9 10

3. How would you rate this person's ability to stay on task for this project?

   1 2 3 4 5 6 7 8 9 10

4. Overall, as a group member, how would you rate this person?

   1 2 3 4 5 6 7 8 9 10

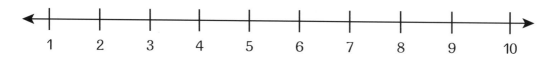

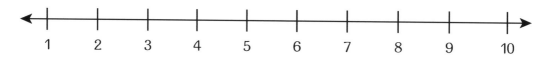

Name: ______________________________ Date: ______________

PRODUCT RUBRIC

Create Your Own Political Party

Political Party:			
Overall	**President:** ____________	**Vice President:** ____________	**Campaign:** ____________
Excellent (A)	◆ President is confident in his or her speech, looking at the audience and speaking clearly. ◆ President covers three issues in their platform, clearly stating where they stand and how they will handle the issue. ◆ President persuades the audience of his or her opinion, using evidence and facts to do so.	◆ Vice president is confident in his or her speech, looking at the audience and speaking clearly. ◆ Vice president covers three issues in their platform, clearly stating where they stand and how they will handle the issue. ◆ Vice president persuades the audience of his or her opinion, using evidence and facts to do so.	◆ Campaign sign has the party name, candidates' names, party slogan, and mascot. ◆ Campaign sign is easy to see and clearly represents what the party stands for. ◆ Campaign itself fits together clearly; the sign, president's speech, and vice president's speech all complement one another.
Good (B–C)	◆ President is confident in his or her speech most of the time, looking at the audience but also looking a lot at notes. ◆ President covers three issues in their platform, but doesn't always clearly state where they stand and how they will handle the issue. ◆ President persuades the audience of his or her opinion occasionally, using evidence and facts to do so, but is not consistent.	◆ Vice president is confident in his or her speech most of the time, looking at the audience but also looking a lot at notes. ◆ Vice president covers three issues in their platform, but doesn't always clearly state where they stand and how they will handle the issue. ◆ Vice president persuades the audience of his or her opinion occasionally, using evidence and facts to do so, but is not consistent.	◆ Campaign sign is missing either the party name, candidates' names, party slogan, or mascot, but not more than one. ◆ Campaign sign can be read but it does not clearly represent what the party stands for. ◆ Campaign itself fits together, but parts of the sign, president's speech, and/or vice president's speech are inconsistent with the overall platform.

Name: ____________________ Date: ____________

Project Rubric: Create Your Own Political Party, *continued*

Overall	**President:** ________	**Vice President:** ________	**Campaign:** ________
Needs Improvement (D–F)	◆ President is not confident in his or her speech, reading notes off the page in a bland manner. ◆ President covers two or fewer issues in their platform, providing almost no detail as to where they stand and how they will handle the issue. ◆ President does not persuade the audience of his or her opinion, having no evidence and facts to do so.	◆ Vice president is not confident in his or her speech, reading notes off the page in a bland manner. ◆ Vice president covers two or fewer issues in their platform, providing almost no detail as to where they stand and how they will handle the issue. ◆ Vice president does not persuade the audience of his or her opinion, having no evidence and facts to do so.	◆ Campaign sign is missing more than two of either the party name, candidates' names, party slogan, or mascot. ◆ Campaign sign is not easy to see or gives no indication of what the party stands for. ◆ Campaign does not fit together; either the sign, president's speech, or vice president's speech is different from the overall platform.

3 Group Discussion

Discussions can take what is being learned to a higher level. There are two types of group discussions. One involves students participating and answering with very surface-level responses. The discussion dies on the vine before it can bloom. It looks like a discussion, but it certainly does not feel like one. There is usually no energy, no passion, and, although you might get the information you seek from students, no depth. The second type of group discussion is one in which students cannot wait to participate because what they want to share is burning a hole in their minds. It may require some content knowledge, but it also requires tapping into experiences and opinions. This is the type of discussion you want to have in your classroom.

What It Looks Like

An easy way to make a group discussion meaningful is to make sure the questions being asked are higher level questions. If you are looking for discussions to generate closed-ended, knowledge-based information, it becomes a hunt-and-peck event, where you are simply looking for someone to provide the correct answer. If, however, the questions are open-ended, higher level questions designed to be cracked open and explored, the discussion will be meaningful. Some of this involves preparing challenging, higher level questions ahead of time. This also means being able to generate these higher level questions in response to what a student has said. It requires a teacher to be able to think quickly on her feet and ask appropriate follow-up questions to mine all of the meaningful lessons from a conversation.

Group discussions do not need to be led by the teacher. Teachers often feel the need to be the ones steering the ship so that it will head in the direction they want it to go in, but sometimes the most interesting trips involve detours. In this case, allowing the discussion to wander to seemingly unrelated topics or to allow students to explore ideas you had not even considered might actually produce better results than you expect. Dividing the students into groups and providing them with a few guiding questions to get the discussion going can lead to these results. Without the teacher there, students might provide more creative answers instead of searching for the answer they believe the teacher is looking for.

Grading a discussion can be a little challenging, but taking copious notes on how a student responds and his level of understanding, or even recording the discussion for you to go back to later are methods you can use to assess a discussion.

What If You Changed the Point of View?

Can you imagine the *The Wonderful Wizard of Oz* told from the perspective of the Wicked Witch of the West or Harry Potter told from the perspective of Snape? How might the story have been different if *Cinderella* was told from the point of view of Prince Charming or if *The Lord of Rings* was seen through the eyes of Sam and not Frodo?

In this project, students will rewrite a well-known story, changing the point of view. How will the story, plot, or perception of characters change as a result? What influence did point of view have on the original story, and how will that change the new version? Students will then read their new story to a group of students and then lead a discussion about how the story changed due to the different point of view. They will then complete the project with a one-on-one reflection with the teacher.

Connections to CCSS

- RL.3.6
- RL.4.6
- RL.5.6
- W.3.3
- W.4.3
- W.5.3
- SL.3.1
- SL.4.1
- SL.5.1

Materials

- Project Outline: What If You Changed the Point of View? (student copies)
- Suggested Timeline
- Lesson: When Point of View Changes
- Lesson: How to Lead a Good Discussion
- Handout 3.1: Peer Review (student copies)
- Handout 3.2: Student Reflection (student copies)
- Discussion Assessment Form (teacher's copies)
- One-on-One Discussion Assessment Form (teacher's copies)
- Product Rubric (student copies)

Supplemental Materials

- *The True Story of the Three Little Pigs* by Jon Scieszka and Lane Smith (teacher's copy)

Name: ______________________________ Date: ________________

PROJECT OUTLINE

What If You Changed the Point of View?

Directions: Can you imagine the *The Wonderful Wizard of Oz* told from the perspective of the Wicked Witch of the West or Harry Potter told from the perspective of Snape? How might the story have been different if *Cinderella* was told from the point of view of Prince Charming or if *The Lord of Rings* was seen through the eyes of Sam and not Frodo?

You will rewrite a well-known story, changing the point of view. How will the story, plot, or perception of characters change as a result? What influence did point of view have on the original story, and how will that change the new version? You will then read your new story to a group of students. Then you will lead a discussion about how the story changed due to the different point of view. You will then complete the project with a one-on-one reflection with your teacher.

You will want to choose a story to rewrite that is familiar to others so that they can compare your version to the original. If you feel you have chosen a story that is not well known, you should be prepared to present the original story as well. Examples of stories you could use include:

- Goldilocks and the Three Bears
- Paul Bunyan
- King Midas and the Golden Touch
- Rumpelstiltskin
- John Henry
- Little Red Riding Hood
- Cinderella
- Princess and the Pea
- Johnny Appleseed
- Billy Goats Gruff
- Chicken Little
- The Emperor's New Clothes
- The Frog Prince
- Jack and the Beanstalk
- Hansel and Gretel

SUGGESTED TIMELINE

DAY 1	2	3	4	5
Conduct Lesson: When Point of View Changes.	Have students choose a story they want to rewrite from another perspective.	Have students begin to write their new stories from the different perspective.	Have students continue to write their new stories from the different perspective.	Have students continue to write their new stories from the different perspective.
6 Have students continue to write their new stories from the different perspective.	**7** Students should finish their stories from a different perspective.	**8** Have students practice reading their story aloud.	**9** Conduct Lesson: How to Have a Good Discussion.	**10** Begin student discussions (see Handout 3.1: Peer Review, Group Discussion Assessment Form).
11 Conduct student discussions.	**12** Conduct student discussions.	**13** Begin one-on-one student reflection discussions (see Handout 3.2: Student Reflection, One-on-One Discussion Assessment Form, Product Rubric).	**14** Conduct one-on-one student reflection discussions.	**15** Conduct one-on-one student reflection discussions.

LESSON

When Point of View Changes

As an introduction and example, read to the class *The True Story of the Three Little Pigs* by Jon Scieszka and Lane Smith. Have a class discussion about what happened to the story when the point of view was changed from the pigs' to the wolf's.

Ask:

1. What was similar about the story?
2. What was different about the story?
3. How did the change in perspective influence how events were described? Provide an example.
4. Do you think the story told is an accurate one? Why or why not? Is it possible to figure out which one is the true story?
5. What if the wolf had not had a cold? How would that change his version of the story?
6. Did you sympathize more with the wolf given that it was from his perspective?
7. What is a third perspective the story could be written from? How might the story change if told from this perspective?
8. Which version of the story do you like better? What are your reasons for this?
9. Have you ever had a situation in your own life where two people had different versions of the same event?
10. How do you think the saying, "truth is in the eye of the beholder," applies to this story?

LESSON

How to Lead a Good Discussion

Share with students the following tips for good discussions:

1. Ask a question that causes people to think because it does not have an obvious answer.
2. Be prepared, have questions written out beforehand.
3. Don't judge the responses (provide a safe environment).
4. Don't let one person dominate the discussion; try to involve all participants.
5. Listen as much if not more than you speak.
6. Be willing to ask follow-up questions to further the conversation.
7. Be enthusiastic about your topic.
8. Summarize important points.

Discussion Days

Tell students that in order to share and discuss their stories they will be broken into groups at stations around the room (e.g., five stations each with someone leading the discussion and an audience). They will be given an allotted amount of time to conduct their discussion and then rotate the audience and speakers until everyone has had multiple chances to lead and take part in a discussion.

After each round of discussion is over, audience members will fill out evaluations for how they felt the discussion went on Handout 3.1: Peer Review. As the teacher, you may want to move about the room and record your observations during discussions.

Name: ______________________________ Date: ______________

HANDOUT 3.1

Peer Review

Directions: Check the box you feel best describes how the student's discussion went.

Peer's Name: ____________________ Peer's Story: ____________________

- ❑ The student asked mostly basic questions that resulted in short, one-sentence answers.
- ❑ The student asked some basic questions that resulted in short answers but from time to time asked a question that sparked some deeper discussion.
- ❑ The student consistently asked questions that caused me to think about the point of view, leading to further discussion but did not ask follow-up questions to expand it.
- ❑ The student consistently asked questions that caused me to think about the point of view, leading to further discussion and follow-up questions that expanded it.

Peer's Name: ____________________ Peer's Story: ____________________

- ❑ The student asked mostly basic questions that resulted in short, one-sentence answers.
- ❑ The student asked some basic questions that resulted in short answers but from time to time asked a question that sparked some deeper discussion.
- ❑ The student consistently asked questions that caused me to think about the point of view, leading to further discussion but did not ask follow-up questions to expand it.
- ❑ The student consistently asked questions that caused me to think about the point of view, leading to further discussion and follow-up questions that expanded it.

Peer's Name: ____________________ Peer's Story: ____________________

- ❑ The student asked mostly basic questions that resulted in short, one-sentence answers.
- ❑ The student asked some basic questions that resulted in short answers but from time to time asked a question that sparked some deeper discussion.
- ❑ The student consistently asked questions that caused me to think about the point of view, leading to further discussion but did not ask follow-up questions to expand it.
- ❑ The student consistently asked questions that caused me to think about the point of view, leading to further discussion and follow-up questions that expanded it.

Name: ______________________________ Date: ______________

HANDOUT 3.2

Student Reflection

Directions: Answer the following reflection questions with lots of detail to support your opinions.

1. What would you give yourself as a grade for this project? Justify your evaluation.

2. What did you like about the project?

3. What did you dislike about the project?

Name: ______________________________ Date: ______________

Handout 3.2: Student Reflection, *continued*

4. If you could change anything about the project, what would it be and why?

5. If you had it to do over again, would you do anything differently? Why?

6. What is one thing you feel you did really well during this project?

7. What did you learn from others during this project?

ASSESSMENT FORM

Discussion

Directions: Put an X or mark where the student is on the scale.

Comprehension	Application	Analysis/ Synthesis	Evaluation
Student has basic understanding but when asked to go deeper he/she struggles to make connections.	Student has a basic understanding and can apply what he/she has learned to a situation but does not bring anything new or insightful to the discussion.	Student has a deeper understanding than just the basics and can build on others' ideas but does not justify decisions with evidence.	Student understands at a deeper level and justifies decisions with sound evidence.

Student's Name: ______________________________

Student's Name: ______________________________

Student's Name: ______________________________

Student's Name: ______________________________

Student's Name: ______________________________

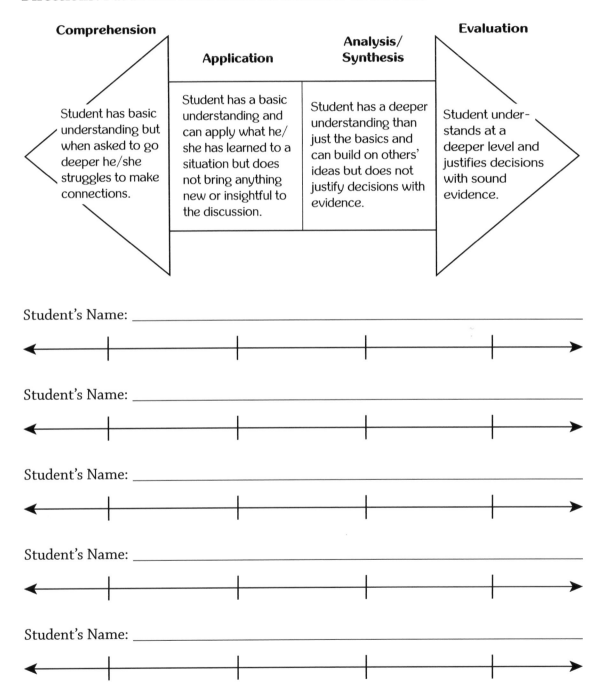

ASSESSMENT FORM

One-on-One Discussion

Directions: Put an X or mark where the student is on the scale.

Comprehension	Application	Analysis/ Synthesis	Evaluation
Student has basic understanding but when asked to go deeper he/she struggles to make connections.	Student has a basic understanding and can apply what he/ she has learned to a situation but does not bring anything new or insightful to the discussion.	Student has a deeper understanding than just the basics and can build on others' ideas but does not justify decisions with evidence.	Student under-stands at a deeper level and justifies decisions with sound evidence.

Student's Name: ____________________

Student's Name: ____________________

Student's Name: ____________________

Student's Name: ____________________

Student's Name: ____________________

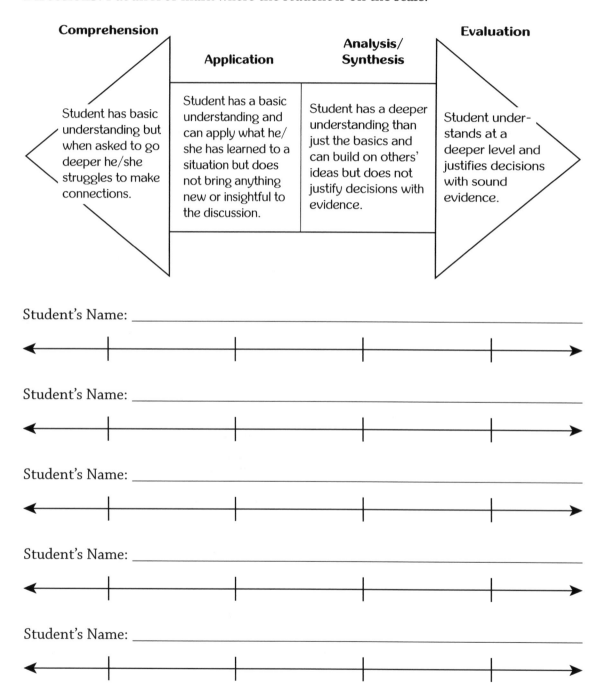

Name: ______________________________ Date: ______________

PRODUCT RUBRIC

What If You Changed the Point of View?

Overall	Point of View	Grammar/Spelling	Story
Excellent (A)	◆ Story is consistently told from the point of view of a different character than the original. ◆ Story clearly describes how speaker's point of view influences events in a natural manner that makes sense.	◆ Story has little to no spelling/grammar errors. ◆ Story is typed in the correct format. ◆ Sentence structure makes the paragraphs flow and easy to read.	◆ Story uses many descriptive details throughout to help set the scene. ◆ It is clear which story it is based on. ◆ There is a clear sequence of events.
Good (B–C)	◆ Story is told from the point of view of a different character than the original but not consistently, showing scenes the character was not present for. ◆ Story describes how speaker's point of view influences events most times in a manner that sometimes does not make sense.	◆ Story has the occasional spelling/grammar error, making more than a handful of mistakes. ◆ Story is typed but not always in the correct format. ◆ Sentence structure mostly makes the paragraphs flow and easy to read, but has the occasional awkward sentence that causes confusion.	◆ Story uses many descriptive details to help set the scene but is not consistent throughout. ◆ It is not immediately clear which story it is based on. ◆ There is a clear sequence of events, but at times it jumps around, causing confusion.
Needs Improvement (D–F)	◆ Story is told from the point of view of a different character than the original, but many of the scenes the character was not present at and wouldn't have been able to tell about them. ◆ Story describes how speaker's point of view influences events that do not make sense with the different perspective.	◆ Story has many spelling/grammar errors, making it difficult to read at times. ◆ Story is typed in a sloppy manner, making it difficult to read. ◆ Sentence structure makes the paragraphs difficult to follow and makes it unclear what is being written about.	◆ Story does not use many descriptive details to set the scene. ◆ It is not clear which story it is based on. ◆ There is not a clear sequence of events, making it difficult to read.

4 Role-Playing

Role-playing is a form of creative oral presentation where a student must inhabit a specific persona and carry out the role from that person's perspective. It allows students to walk a day in the shoes of someone else and helps them to understand different perspectives. A constant struggle with students is to get them to think about anything from another perspective than their own. Giving them opportunities to explore other perspectives will allow them to gain a better understanding of a character, time period, or idea.

What It Looks Like

Role-playing can involve having a person assume the role of a character from a novel to demonstrate how he would react to situations the character had to experience. Or it can involve a mock trial in which a student is given a specific role to play such as a lawyer, a witness, a defendant, the judge, or even the jury. Although a student is focusing in on her specific role, she is getting an understanding of how a trial works and of the arguments being made.

It's a Mystery

Detectives use scientific deductive reasoning in order to solve crimes, figuring out what does not belong or what stands out. All suspects and motives must be considered until the mystery is figured out.

In this project, students will be divided into groups and will write and stage their own mystery for others to try and solve, leaving clues and evidence to allow them to put it together and come up with a solution.

Connections to CCSS

- W.3.3
- W.4.3
- W.5.3
- SL.3.2
- SL.4.2
- SL.5.2

Materials

- Project Outline: It's a Mystery (student copies)
- Suggested Timeline
- Lesson: How to Conduct a Mystery
- Handout 4.1: Investigation Into Mr. Rockwell's Kidnapping (student copies)
- Product Rubric (student copies)

Supplemental Materials

- Encyclopedia Brown books (teacher's copies)
- Materials for staging Mr. Rockwell's Kidnapping:
  - An alarm clock set to 2:30 p.m.
  - Two cups, one with lipstick on it
  - A pill bottle labeled "diabetes medication"

Name: ______________________________ Date: ______________

PROJECT OUTLINE

It's a Mystery

Directions: Detectives use scientific deductive reasoning in order to solve crimes, figuring out what does not belong or what stands out. All suspects and motives must be considered until the mystery is figured out.

Your group will write and stage your own mystery for others to try and solve, leaving clues and evidence to allow them to put it together and come up with a solution. You will need to create three suspects, which you and your team members will portray. You will provide clues and construct a crime scene that allows others to try and solve the crime. Make sure the mystery is challenging but not impossible.

Your scene must include:

- three suspects who could be guilty, including well-thought-out backgrounds and personalities;
- evidence that points in one suspect's direction (you can only have one guilty party);
- other evidence that might make the other suspects seem guilty (red herring);
- alibis for all suspects except the guilty one; and
- props that set the crime scene.

SUGGESTED TIMELINE

DAY				
1 Introduce the proj-ect, conduct Lesson: How to Conduct a Mystery, and distribute Handout 4.1.	**2** Have students brainstorm ideas for their mystery. Finish class by reading a mystery from *Encyclopedia Brown*.	**3** Have students brainstorm ideas for their mystery. Finish class by reading a mystery from *Encyclopedia Brown*.	**4** Have students begin to create their mystery. Finish class by reading a mystery from *Encyclopedia Brown*.	**5** Have students continue to create their mystery. Finish class by reading a mystery from *Encyclopedia Brown*.
6 Have students continue to create their mystery.	**7** Have students finish creating their mystery.	**8** Students need to bring in their evidence/props and learn their parts.	**9** Have students practice their mysteries.	**10** Have groups present, while the rest of the class tries to solve the mysteries.

LESSON

How to Conduct a Mystery

Conduct your own mystery, having the students participate and modeling the type of mysteries they will be writing and presenting. You can use the mystery provided or create your own.

Mr. Rockwell's Kidnapping

You will need:

- An alarm clock set to 2:30 p.m.
- Two cups, one with lipstick on it
- A pill bottle labeled "diabetes medication"

Arrange the scene as though a struggle has occurred. Distribute Handout 4.1 and give students 10–15 minutes to look over the scene and read the clues. Everything they will need to solve the crime is available in the scene or in the clues. Tell students:

It's June 29. Maximus Rockwell, the famous software engineer, has been kidnapped from his estate. The police were called at 5 p.m. and you have just arrived half an hour later. The room is exactly like it was found by police, and nothing has been allowed to enter since the kidnapper left the room. There are five suspects, all staff members of Mr. Rockwell. There is the butler, the maid, the cook, the driver, and the personal assistant. All of them have been interviewed and their statements are available on Handout 4.1. You must figure out which of them is guilty of kidnapping Mr. Rockwell and what evidence leads you to this. Mr. Rockwell's life depends on it.

Solution

After students have completed their investigation, share the solution with them.

When: The crime was committed at 3 p.m. You can tell because the alarm clock is displaying 2:30 but the current time is 5:30. Obviously the cord was unplugged in the struggle and plugged back in. Because the clock resets at 12:00, it means the crime was committed 2.5 hours ago, putting it at 3 p.m.

Who: Julie, Mr. Rockwell's personal assistant, committed the kidnapping. The fact that the glass has lipstick on it means it was done by a woman. If the crime was committed 2.5 hours ago, it could only be the cook or the personal assistant because the maid was not in town. Between the cook and the personal assistant, the cook could not have written the note that is typed because she doesn't know how to use a computer, not liking technology. That means Julie is the one who did it.

Why: Mr. Rockwell was contacting his lawyer, as evidenced by the appointment in his calendar. He was going to rewrite his will and put the driver in it, maybe cutting out all of the others. The secretary knew about this because she sets up all his appointments. She kidnapped Mr. Rockwell before he could write another draft of the will.

End-of-Day Activity

Get a copy of any Encyclopedia Brown book by Donald Sobol (there are 29 of them), which have short mysteries you can read to the class that they can try and solve to give them a better understanding of how a mystery is set up. These tend to be age appropriate and do not have violence like other similar mysteries.

- *Encyclopedia Brown, Boy Detective*
- *Encyclopedia Brown Finds the Clues*
- *Encyclopedia Brown Tracks Them Down*
- *Encyclopedia Brown Takes the Case*
- *Encyclopedia Brown Cracks the Case*

Day of Mysteries

Tell students that after groups have created their mysteries they will present them. As a group presents its mystery, the rest of the class will observe and try and solve it in their groups. The group running the scene will introduce its mystery and its characters. Students will spend about 10–15 minutes at each scene—7 minutes to survey the scene and ask questions to the suspects, 3 minutes as a group to try and put it all together, and 5 minutes for groups to report out their guesses and for the group running the scene to reveal their guilty party and the evidence that led to this. Students will then move on to the next group's scene.

Name: ______________________ Date: ______________

HANDOUT 4.1

Investigation Into Mr. Rockwell's Kidnapping

Last Will and Testament

I bequeath all of my worldly possessions to be divided amongst my staff. This should be done equally.

The staff includes:

- Patty Underwood
- Ken Jones
- Julie Havens
- Andrea Green

Signed,

Maximus Rockwell

Maximus Rockwell
August 15, 2016

RANSOM NOTE

Maximus Rockwell has been kidnapped. If you ever want to see him alive, you will pay me $5 million and leave it by the brook on the south side of the estate.

If you contact the police, I will have no choice but to kill Mr. Rockwell. This is not a joke.

Name: ______________________________ Date: ______________

Handout 4.1: Investigation Into Mr. Rockwell's Kidnapping, *continued*

Mr. Rockwell's Agenda

June 29:

Board of Directors 11:00
Tennis 1:00
Lunch 2:30
Doctor's appointment 3:45
Meet with the lawyer 6:00
Dinner with Andre 8:30
Conference call 10:15

Witness Statements

Patty Underwood—Maid

Patty has worked for Mr. Rockwell for the past 15 years. She has been one of his most loyal staff members. She is an aspiring author, writing romance novels in her spare time. She spent most of the afternoon shopping at the store in town from 1:30–3:30 p.m. She spent the rest of the afternoon doing laundry in the basement.

Ken Jones—Butler

The butler is a former boxer and has always had a little bit of a temper. He was once almost fired for getting into a fight with the driver. He has always been loyal to Mr. Rockwell, however, and works around the clock to serve him. Because of this he rarely leaves the mansion if Mr. Rockwell is home. When he could not find Mr. Rockwell he called the police.

Darren Piper—Driver

Darren is a fairly new employee, only hired in the past year or so. He apparently saved Mr. Rockwell's life a couple of months ago when Mr. Rockwell had a seizure from lack of medication. Darren performed CPR until the ambulance arrived. He was getting the car fixed at the garage from 2–4 p.m.

Name: ______________________________ Date: ______________

Handout 4.1: Investigation Into Mr. Rockwell's Kidnapping, *continued*

Julie Havens—Personal Assistant

Julie is the personal assistant to Mr. Rockwell, setting up all of his appointments and business dealings. She is a wiz with electronics and very organized, both plusses in her line of work. She was running some errands from 3:30–5 p.m.

Andrea Green—Cook

Andrea spent most of the day in the kitchen making pies for dinner. She says she didn't hear anything. She does not like technology of any kind and prefers to cook with an old-fashioned wood-burning stove. She had to go to the grocery store to get supplies from 1:30–2:30 p.m.

Name: ______________________________ Date: ______________

PRODUCT RUBRIC

It's a Mystery

Overall	Performance	Scene	Mystery
Excellent (A)	◆ Group created three suspects, who had distinctive roles and different perspectives, as well as colorful personalities. ◆ Members stayed in character and were creative in their portrayal. ◆ Members conveyed information through their characters that was easy to understand and could be used to solve the mystery.	◆ Mystery was staged to represent a crime scene, with details that brought the scene to life. ◆ Group used multiple effective props to set the scene and that could be used to help solve the mystery. ◆ Scene was clearly set by the descriptive summary the group provided, introducing the victim, the suspects, and the scenario.	◆ Mystery was engaging and told a clear story. ◆ Mystery presented multiple pieces of evidence that could be used to solve it. ◆ Solution to the mystery makes sense, and, although not impossible, it was a challenge for others to solve.
Good (B–C)	◆ Group created three suspects, who had something to do with the case, but they were not distinctive or colorful personalities. ◆ Members stayed in character, breaking only occasionally from their parts, and were creative in their portrayal. ◆ Members conveyed information through their characters that was mostly easy to understand, but there were times when the portrayal was confusing.	◆ Mystery was staged to represent a crime scene but did not have many details. ◆ Group used one effective prop to set the scene that could be used to help solve the mystery. ◆ Scene was set by the summary the group provided, although it could be more descriptive, introducing the victim, the suspects, and the scenario.	◆ Mystery was engaging, but sometimes the story was confusing. ◆ Mystery presented evidence that could be used to solve it. ◆ Solution to the mystery makes sense but was fairly easy to solve.
Needs Improvement (D–F)	◆ Group created three suspects, who have did not have distinctive roles or perspectives, and it was difficult to tell one suspect from another. ◆ Members often did not stay in character, forgetting they were playing a part. ◆ Members conveyed information through their characters that was not easy to understand and did not really help in solving the mystery.	◆ There were no attempts to represent a crime scene. ◆ Group did not use any effective props to set the scene or that could be used to help solve the mystery. ◆ Summary the group provided did not introduce the victim, the suspects, and/or the scenario.	◆ Mystery was boring and did not tell a clear story. ◆ Mystery did not present evidence that could be used to solve it. ◆ Solution to the mystery makes no sense or it was impossible to solve.

5 Interview

Students often imagine teachers as the expert of their disciplines. If you are a language arts teacher, you are expected to be able to spell every single word in the English language correctly or to have read every book in the library. If you are a math teacher, you should know how to solve any math problem or know all of the mathematical principles that govern the discipline.

We as teachers know the truth: There are times when we simply do not know the answer, or we are teaching a topic we are not comfortable with. Having students interview an expert on a topic is a good learning tool that provides a real-world connection. Not only that, unlike using a book or the Internet to find an answer, the students can ask exactly what it is they want to know and receive an instant answer. There is no inferring or reading between the lines. It is a direct way to get content and insight about a topic.

What It Looks Like

Interviews can be done in a couple of ways. One way is for the student herself to locate an expert in a topic she wants to know more about and conduct an individual interview. The interview is tailored to this student's needs and she gains valuable information from the source.

A second way to conduct an interview is for the teacher to bring in an expert or panel of experts for the students to question. There does need to be a format to this process. You do not want to just turn students loose to ask any questions that come to mind. Students might ask off-topic questions or even inappropriate ones, and time that could have been spent getting valuable insight from the speaker is wasted. Bringing in an expert can take the learning to a deeper, more meaningful level.

Message in a Bottle

In this project, students will become an international pen pal with someone from a different country. This can be done over the Internet. They will carry on a correspondence with this person over an extended period of time, getting to know who he or she is. They must ask questions about his or her likes/dislikes, culture, and other interests. They will collect this correspondence in a paper or electronic portfolio, which will be evaluated based on the writing. They will eventually create a trifold poster and profile about their pen pal and his or her culture to share with others as part of a culture fair.

Connections to CCSS

- W.3.4
- W.3.6
- W.4.4
- W.4.6
- W.5.4
- W.5.6
- L.3.1
- L.3.2
- L.4.1
- L.4.2
- L.5.1
- L.5.2

Materials

- Project Outline: Message in a Bottle (student copies)
- Suggested Timeline
- Lesson: How to Write an E-mail
- Handout 5.1: How to Write a Proper E-mail (student copies)
- Product Rubric (student copies)

Name: ______________________________ Date: ________________

PROJECT OUTLINE

Message in a Bottle

Directions: There are students just like you all over the world. Even though they are from different countries whose cultures seem very different from yours, there are cultural universals that make you very much alike.

You will become an international pen pal with someone from a different country. This can be done over the Internet. You will carry on a correspondence with this person over an extended period of time, getting to know who he or she is. You must ask questions about his or her likes/dislikes, culture, and other interests. You will collect this correspondence in a paper or electronic portfolio, which will be evaluated based on the writing. You will eventually create a trifold poster and profile about your pen pal and his or her culture to share with others as part of a culture fair.

Your trifold should profile the person you corresponded with on the left panel and profile the country that person is from on the right panel. You should include your e-mail correspondence in the middle panel.

SUGGESTED TIMELINE

WEEK
1 Introduce the project and conduct Lesson: How to Write an E-mail.
2 Students should have identified someone from a foreign country they can correspond with and have written two e-mails to them.
3 Students should write their third e-mail.
4 Students should write their fourth e-mail.
5 Students should write their fifth e-mail.
6 Students should write their sixth e-mail.
7 Students should write their seventh e-mail.
8 Students should write their eighth e-mail.
9 Students should work on their trifold for the culture fair and write a ninth e-mail.
10 Students should present their trifolds at a culture fair.

LESSON

How to Write an E-mail

Using a free resource such as epals (http://www.epals.com), have students set up a correspondence with a student from a foreign country. Over the course of several weeks, students must correspond with their counterpart 8–10 times. Students will be interviewing their pen pal to find out both the likes/dislikes and personal interests of their pen pal, as well as the culture of their pen pal through questioning and correspondence. Distribute Handout 5.1: How to Write a Proper E-mail and review the tips with students.

Students should correspond with their pen pal once a week. Their correspondence will be evaluated on writing conventions, such as grammar, spelling, capitalization, and clarity. Students will collect their correspondence, as well as information about their pen pal's life and culture, on a trifold to be presented at the culture fair at the end of the project. You can invite parents and community members to the culture fair to see what students have learned about the culture of the person who is their pen pal.

Name: ______________________________ Date: ______________

HANDOUT 5.1

How to Write a Proper E-mail

1. **Use a short, accurate heading for your e-mail.** Consider a subject such as: *Pen pal from America, Wanting to learn about your country,* or *Hoping we can become pen pals.*

2. **Begin with a proper salutation.** *Dear (first name, last name) . . .*

3. **Introduce yourself.** *My name is ______. I am a fourth grader from Dover, DE, and I attend James K. Polk Elementary.*

4. **Communicate your message.** *I am working on a project where I need to learn about the culture of someone from another country. I was hoping to ask you questions about your country in order to learn more about it for the project.*

5. **End with a salutation.** *Sincerely, Respectfully, Cordially.*

6. **Check that your content communicates what you want it to clearly.** Read it aloud in order to catch content errors. You might even want to read it to someone else to see if they understand what you are trying to communicate.

7. **Check spelling/grammar.** Make sure there are no spelling errors, you use proper capitalization, and that it is grammatically correct. You are going to be graded on this so treat it as a professional piece of writing.

8. **Send your e-mail.** If you do not receive a response in a few days, send a follow-up e-mail to make sure your pen pal received it. If you still do not receive a response you will want to consider trying to find another pen pal.

9. **Maintain professionalism.** Even once you get to know your pen pal and have established a relationship with him or her, make sure to stay professional in your e-mails.

Name: ______________________________ Date: ______________

PRODUCT RUBRIC

Message in a Bottle

Overall	Clarity	Grammar/Spelling	Responsibility
Excellent (A)	• E-mails use sentence structure that makes the paragraphs flow and easy to read. • Most of the questions asked are appropriate and are designed to get much detail and explanation from the recipient.	• Correspondence has little to no spelling/grammar errors. • Correspondence uses capitalization correctly consistently. • Correspondence is typed in the correct format.	• There are 8–10 pieces of correspondence. • Each e-mail is at least a page long. • E-mails were sent weekly.
Good (B–C)	• E-mails mostly uses sentence structure that makes the paragraphs flow and easy to read but has the occasional awkward sentence that causes confusion. • Many of the questions asked are appropriate and are designed to get much detail and explanation from the recipient, but there are a few that are not clear or would produce a one- or two-word answer.	• Correspondence has occasional spelling/grammar errors. • Correspondence uses capitalization correctly but not always consistently. • Most of the correspondence is typed in the correct format, but a few are not in proper letter format.	• There are 5–7 pieces of correspondence. • Most e-mails are at least a page long but a few are shorter. • E-mails were sent weekly for the most part.
Needs Improvement (D–F)	• E-mails have sloppy sentence structure that makes the paragraphs difficult to follow and unclear. • Most of the questions asked are not appropriate or clear ones designed to get much detail and explanation from the recipient.	• Correspondence has many spelling/grammar errors. • Correspondence does not use capitalization correctly consistently. • Much of the correspondence is not in proper letter format.	• There are less than five pieces of correspondence. • Most e-mails are shorter than a page long. • E-mails were not sent weekly.

Name: ______________________________ Date: ________________

PRODUCT RUBRIC

Culture Fair

Overall	Professionalism	Profile of Pen Pal	Profile of Country
Excellent (A)	• Trifold has little to no spelling/grammar errors. • Items on the trifold are organized clearly, using headings and large enough print. • Trifold is neat, bright, and catches the eye.	• There are five or more photos showing the pen pal and his or her interests and hobbies. • Trifold clearly communicates the pen pal's life, including his or her likes/dislikes, family, friends, and hobbies.	• There are five or more photos showing the culture of the country the pen pal is from. • Trifold includes a clear map of the country that shows exactly where the pen pal lives. • Trifold provides a clear understanding of what the culture is like in the pen pal's country and how it is similar/different than the U.S.
Good (B–C)	• Trifold has a few minor spelling/grammar errors. • Most of the items on the trifold are organized clearly, but there are not consistent headings or the print is too small. • Trifold is neat but looks sort of plain.	• There are three or four photos of the pen pal and his or her interests and hobbies. • Trifold communicates the pen pal's likes/dislikes, family, friends, and hobbies, although it is not always clear or important information is missing.	• There are three or four photos showing the culture of the country the pen pal is from. • Trifold includes a map of the country that shows where the pen pal lives, but it is small and hard to make out. • Leaves one with an understanding of what the culture is like in the country but not how it is similar/different than the U.S.
Needs Improvement (D–F)	• Trifold has many spelling/grammar errors. • Items on the trifold are not organized, making it difficult to follow. • Trifold is sloppy and unprofessional.	• There are two or fewer photos of the pen pal and his or her interests and hobbies. • Trifold does not communicate the pen pal's life, including his or her likes/dislikes, family, friends, and hobbies.	• There are two or fewer photos showing the culture of the country the pen pal is from. • Trifold does not include clear map of the country that shows exactly where the pen pal lives or the map is difficult to see. • Trifold does not provide a clear understanding of what the culture is like in the country and how it is similar/different than the U.S.

6 Exhibition

An exhibition is an exhibit of what the students have learned. An audience usually views the exhibition, whether it is made up of other students in the class, other classes from the school, parents, or outside audience members. The tricky thing about an exhibition is that the students cannot explain themselves orally; they must let the work explain itself. The analogy I often use with students when demonstrating an exhibition is the telling of a joke: "Two guys walk into a bar. The third one ducks." Nearly every time I tell this joke, I get puzzled looks and furrowed brows. I always feel a need to explain the joke: "You see, the bar in this case is not an establishment where one purchases alcohol. The bar is an actual metal bar that the people physically walk into . . ."

It's hilarious, right? Wrong. Because I have to explain the joke, it is not funny (no matter how much I think it is). Exhibitions are the exact same way. If you have to verbally explain the exhibit, the exhibit is not accomplishing what it is supposed to. When you go to an art exhibition, the artist is not there to explain what she did and why she did it. The piece has to stand on its own merits.

What It Looks Like

How a student approaches an exhibition is very different from other PBAs. Let us say for the sake of argument that a student creates a trifold as a product. If the student were using an oral presentation as this performance assessment, he might have a few meaningful visuals such as photos or graphs to enhance his explanation. He would not write out everything he plans to say on the board. Otherwise, he will feel compelled to read it verbatim and give a very stiff oral presentation. In an exhibition, the explanation would need to be written out because there is no one there to orally explain it.

An exhibition can come in many forms. A few common ones include:

- trifold,
- poster,
- PowerPoint presentation,
- short story/poem,
- video,
- piece of artwork or a craft, or
- photography series.

No matter which form a student chooses, first and foremost it must inform the audience and allow it to learn from the exhibition.

You Could Be the Next S. E. Hinton

S. E. Hinton was just 16 years old when she wrote her first novel, *The Outsiders*. Anyone of any age can write a book. In this project, students will write a short story and, after editing and workshopping, will submit a final draft and a cover letter to a real-life publication that publishes kids' work.

Connections to CCSS

- W.3.3
- W.3.4
- W.3.5
- W.4.3
- W.4.4
- W.4.5
- W.5.3
- W.5.4
- W.5.5
- L.3.3
- L.4.3
- L.5.3
- L.5.3.A

Materials

- Project Outline: You Could Be the Next S. E. Hinton (student copies)
- Suggested Timeline
- Lesson: Writing Workshop
- Handout 6.1: Basic Story Structure (student copies)
- Handout 6.2: ABC Story (student copies)
- Handout 6.3: Peer Review (student copies)
- Handout 6.4: Completing the Final Draft (student copies)
- Handout 6.5: Writing a Cover Letter (student copies)
- Product Rubric (student copies)

Name: ______________________________ Date: ______________

PROJECT OUTLINE

You Could Be the Next S. E. Hinton

Directions: S. E. Hinton was just 16 years old when she wrote her first novel, *The Outsiders*. Anyone of any age can write a book. You will write a short story and, after editing and workshopping, will submit a final draft and a cover letter to a real-life publication that publishes kids' work.

Story Topics

Consider one of the following to write a story about.

- **Fiction for Beginning Readers** (Ages 6–8, up to 500 words)
  - Humorous stories
  - Folktales
  - Holiday stories
  - Sports stories

- **Fiction for Independent Readers** (Ages 8–12, up to 800 words)
  - Adventure stories
  - Historical fiction
  - Holiday stories
  - Mystery stories

Possible Publications

There are a number of publications that publish kids' work. You may know of one or may be interested in one of the following. Submission guidelines for each vary.

- *Highlights for Kids* (https://www.highlightskids.com/your-own-pages)
- *Stone Soup* (http://www.stonesoup.com)
- *New Moon Girls* (http://newmoon.com/how-to-get-published-new-moon-girls)
- *Creative Kids* (http://www.ckmagazine.org/submissions)
- *The Writers' Slate* (http://www.writingconference.com/writer's.htm)
- *Cricket* (https://cricketmag.submittable.com/submit/17789)

SUGGESTED TIMELINE

DAY 1	2	3	4	5
Introduce the project and review story structure (see Handout 6.1).	Have students begin to brainstorm ideas for their story and practice writing a story (see Handout 6.2).	Have students begin writing a rough draft of their story.	Have students continue writing a rough draft of their story.	Have students continue writing a rough draft of their story.
6	**7**	**8**	**9**	**10**
Have students complete writing a rough draft of their story.	Conduct Lesson: Writing Workshop. Have students workshop their rough draft (see Handout 6.3).	Have students workshop their rough draft.	Have students begin to type a final draft of their story (see Handout 6.4).	Students should continue typing a final draft of their story.
11	**12**	**13**	**14**	**15**
Students should continue typing a final draft of their story.	Students should continue typing a final draft of their story.	Students should continue typing a final draft of their story.	Have students write cover letters (see Handout 6.5).	Have students send their stories for publication.

LESSON

Writing Workshop

Have students form groups of five. Each student will get an allotted time to workshop his or her piece. Students providing feedback need to jot down notes during the reading and offer specific feedback for how to improve the story on Handout 6.3: Peer Review.

After reading his or her piece aloud, the writer will remain silent and take notes during steps 1–4, as peers share their feedback. You will be the timekeeper for this activity.

1. What is the piece about? Summarize the piece. **(1 minute)**

2. What do you think the author is trying to say? What is his or her intent? **(3 minutes)**

3. What do you like about the piece? What is your "must keep"? **(7 minutes)**

4. Ideas for revision: What is not working or do you want more of? **(7 minutes)**

5. Reflective writing: Everyone (writer and peers) write reflectively. Focus on what you learned or what ideas/thoughts about writing you had during the conversation. **(4 minutes)**

6. Writer's response: Writer shares reaction to the feedback. He or she may ask questions of the group or invite them into the conversation. **(6 minutes)**

7. Reaction go-round: Each person gives a short (1–2 sentence) response to what they learned from the workshop. **(2 minutes)**

Name: ______________________ Date: ______________

HANDOUT 6.1

Basic Story Structure

Directions: Use this structure to plot out your story. Remember every story has three elements:

1. Conflict/Crisis
2. Climax
3. Conclusion

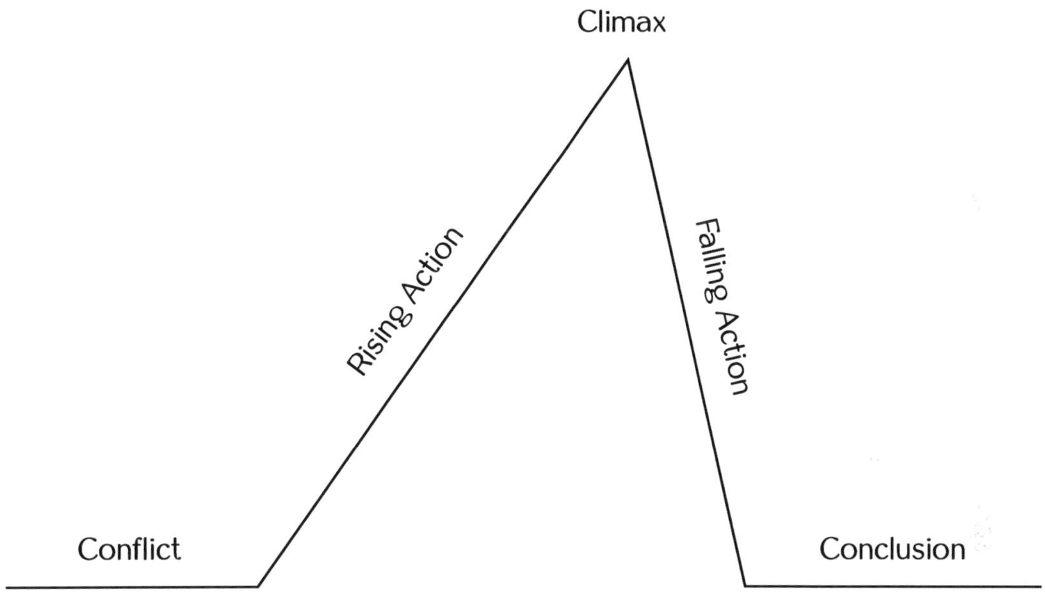

Name: ______________________________ Date: ________________

HANDOUT 6.2

ABC Story

Directions: One challenge facing every fiction writer is how to begin. What should the first sentence of my story be? How do I start? Try this format.

1. Write a 26-sentence story. Make your first sentence begin with an "A" word, your second sentence with a "B" word, and so on.

2. *Make something happen* in those 26 sentences. Your story must have a beginning, a middle (climax), and an end.

3. The goal of the ABC Story is *not* to write a prize-winning, polished story. The goal *is* to get the story down on paper. Stick to the format.

Name: ______________________________ Date: ______________

HANDOUT 6.3

Peer Review

Directions: Be sure to provide as many suggestions as possible. The more information you provide, the better the author will be able to revise.

Peer's Name: ____________________ Peer's Story Title: ____________________

1. What is this piece about? Write a one-sentence summary.

2. What do you think the author is trying to say or do in this piece? What is his or her intent?

3. What are some things about the piece you really like? These may be characters, words/phrases, scenes, or other elements. Put a star next to one *must keep* item.

4. Share ideas for revision. What is not working for you? What do you want more of?

Name: ______________________________ Date: ______________

HANDOUT 6.4

Completing the Final Draft

Directions: Before submitting your story for publication, you will want to be sure it is formatted correctly and well edited. Some publications may have suggested formats for submission. If the publication you are submitting to does not, you may want to follow the basic formatting tips below. You will also want to follow the editing checklist.

Formatting Tips

1. Put the story's title, centered in all caps, approximately one-third of the way down the page.
2. Skip a line and write "by" in lowercase, then skip another line and put your name in all caps.
3. Drop four lines, indent, and begin your story.
4. Use size 12 font, Times New Roman, double-spaced.
5. Print must be on one side of the page.
6. Check for spelling errors or grammatical mistakes.
7. Use a one-inch margin on all sides.

Name: ______________________________ Date: ________________

Handout 6.4: Completing the Final Draft, *continued*

Editing Checklist

- ❑ The conflict, climax, and conclusion can clearly be identified.
- ❑ The characters are believable.
- ❑ The point of view is consistent.
- ❑ The tense (past, present, future) is consistent.
- ❑ The setting is clear.
- ❑ The piece is free from spelling and grammatical errors.
- ❑ The story is descriptive.
- ❑ The story shows the actions, does not tell.
- ❑ Can any short, choppy sentences be improved by combining them?
- ❑ Can any long, awkward sentences be improved by breaking them down into shorter ones?
- ❑ Do you have any run-on sentences?

Name: ______________________________ Date: ______________

HANDOUT 6.5

Writing a Cover Letter

Directions: Here are the different sections of the cover letter. Make sure all of them are addressed and clear.

1. Address the recipient.
2. State why you are writing this letter.
3. Explain the reason for your request.
4. Including a brief synopsis and the word count or your story.
5. Give a little background about yourself.
6. Try to find a connection between you and the person to whom you are writing.
7. Express your appreciation.
8. Make a response as simple as possible by including information needed to get a hold of you.
9. If appropriate, include a self-addressed, stamped envelope.

Name: ______________________________ Date: ______________

Handout 6.5: Writing a Cover Letter, *continued*

Sample Cover Letter

Dear Joëlle Dujardin, Senior Editor:

I am writing about the possible publication of my story in your publication. Enclosed is my short story entitled "Goldilocks and the Three Bears." It tells the story of Goldilocks who is lost in the woods and stumbles across the house of the three bears who are out for a walk. Being hungry, she samples their porridge. Being tired, she rests in their beds and falls asleep. When the three bears come home and find someone has trespassed in their house, they are not happy. The story is aimed at young kids, grades 1–3. I think this story fits in nicely with your magazine, whose main audience is 6–8 years of age.

I am a fourth-grade student at Lincoln Elementary in Texarkana, AR. I have never had anything published but get straight A's in Language Arts and hope someday to be a writer full-time. I am a big fan of J. K. Rowling and the Harry Potter books and aspire to be like her.

I look forward to hearing from you in regard to my story. If you have any questions, do not hesitate to e-mail.

Thank you for your consideration,

The Brothers Grimm
9567 Gingerbread House
Texarkana, AR 83147
brothersgrimm@grimmmail.com

Name: ______________________ Date: ______________

PRODUCT RUBRIC

You Could Be the Next S. E. Hinton

Overall	Clarity	Grammar/Spelling	Revision
Excellent (A)	◆ Story has a clear beginning, middle, and end with clear sequencing. ◆ Story consistently shows with descriptive words and sentences rather than tells. ◆ Sentence structure is clear and easy to follow.	◆ Story has little to no spelling/grammar errors. ◆ Story uses capitalization correctly consistently. ◆ Story is typed in the correct format.	◆ Student turned in both a rough draft and a final draft, along with detailed notes from the workshop. ◆ Student made several good revisions to the final draft based on the information received in the workshop. ◆ Between the rough and final draft, student was consistently able to expand, combine, and reduce sentences for meaning, reader/listener interest, and style.
Good (B–C)	◆ Story has a beginning, middle, and end, but the sequencing is not always clear. ◆ Story shows with descriptive words and sentences rather than tells, but there are a couple of occasions where action is told. ◆ Sentence structure is clear and easy to follow, but there are a few instances where it is confusing.	◆ Story has occasional spelling/grammar errors. ◆ Story uses capitalization correctly but not always consistently. ◆ Most of the story is typed in the correct format, but a few guidelines are not followed.	◆ Student turned in both a rough draft and a final draft, along with sparse notes taken from the workshop. ◆ Student made revisions to the final draft based on the information received in the workshop but overlooked some that needed to be made. ◆ Between the rough and final draft, student was able to expand, combine, and reduce sentences for meaning, reader/listener interest, and style, but is not consistent.
Needs Improvement (D–F)	◆ Story does not have a beginning, middle, and end because the sequencing is not very clear. ◆ Story does not show with descriptive words and sentences; instead it tells the story. ◆ Sentence structure makes the story difficult to follow.	◆ Story has many spelling/grammar errors and is difficult to read. ◆ Story does not use capitalization correctly consistently. ◆ Much of the story is not in proper format as laid out by the guidelines.	◆ Student turned in both a rough draft and a final draft without notes from the workshop. ◆ Student made little to no revisions to the final draft based on the workshop. ◆ Between the rough and final draft, student did not expand, combine, and reduce sentences for meaning, reader/listener interest, and style.

7 Essay

Essays are often thought of only for use in language arts class, but essays can be used for any subject area concerning any topic. An essay basically asks a student to explain what she has learned in written form. You would think this would simply be a translation of what the student is thinking into words, but that is easier said than done. Many students have difficulty making this translation, so it is important to teach writing in all subject areas so that students become familiar with how to make this translation.

What It Looks Like

Essays have a basic five-part structure:

1. **Thesis statement:** This explains the purpose of the essay. It can be thought of as an introduction, but the thesis should be reiterated throughout the essay. It should be strong enough to be able to be backed up with three pieces of evidence.
2. **Evidence 1:** This lays out the evidence that proves the thesis with supporting details. This might be an example from the text (language arts), an example problem (math or science), or a citation of a specific event that backs the thesis (social studies).
3. **Evidence 2:** This is the same as Evidence 1, but with a second example.

4. **Evidence 3:** This is the same as Evidence 1 and 2, but with a third example.
5. **Conclusion:** This summarizes the main thesis and the arguments made. Lots of gifted students like to skip this step because they think they are just repeating themselves. It is safest to assume nothing about the reader and be as clear as possible.

Greatest Historical Mysteries

Who built Stonehenge? Why did the Ancient Mayans abandon their cities? What causes so many planes and ships to disappear in the Bermuda Triangle? These are a few of thousands of historical mysteries that humanity has been trying to solve for thousands of years.

In this project, students will choose a historical mystery to investigate, looking at three possible theories to explain it. They must communicate these theories in an essay and then choose which one they believe is the most plausible, justifying their choice.

Connections to CCSS

- RI. 3.2
- RI.3.6
- RI.3.8
- RI.4.2
- RI.4.6
- RI.4.8
- RI.5.2
- RI.5.6
- RI.5.8
- W.3.1
- W.3.8
- W.4.1
- W.4.8
- W.4.9
- W.5.1
- W.5.8
- W.5.9

Materials

- Project Outline: Greatest Historical Mysteries (student copies)
- Suggested Timeline
- Lesson: How to Conduct Historical Mysteries
- Handout 7.1: Structure of the Essay (student copies)

- Handout 7.2: Research Notes (student copies)
- Handout 7.3: Peer Review (student copies)
- Product Rubric (student copies)

Name: ______________________ Date: ______________

PROJECT OUTLINE

Greatest Historical Mysteries

Directions: Who built Stonehenge? Why did the Ancient Mayans abandon their cities? What causes so many planes and ships to disappear in the Bermuda Triangle? These are a few of thousands of historical mysteries that humanity has been trying to solve for thousands of years.

You will choose a historical mystery to investigate, looking at three possible theories to explain it. You must communicate these theories in an essay and then choose which one you believe is the most plausible, justifying your choice.

Examples of Historical Mysteries

- Extinction of the Dinosaurs
- Atlantis
- Big Foot
- Loch Ness Monster
- Disappearance of the Mayans
- Man in the Iron Mask
- Bermuda Triangle
- Area 51
- Easter Island
- King Tut's death
- Lemuria
- Crystal Skulls
- Lost City of Gold
- Petra
- Nabta Playa
- Movement of Antarctica
- Iron Pillar
- Stone Spheres of Costa Rica
- Baghdad Battery
- Pyramid of Giza
- Newport Tower
- Derinkuyu
- Mary Celeste
- Bimini Road
- Klerksdorp Spheres
- Fountain of Youth
- Nazca Lines
- Piri Reis Map
- Great Zimbabwe
- Disappearance of Amelia Earhart
- Voynich Manuscript
- Crop Circles
- Hollow Earth
- Lost Colony of Roanoke

SUGGESTED TIMELINE

DAY				
1 Introduce project and conduct Lesson: Introduction to Historical Mysteries.	**2** Review the basic structure of an essay (see Handout 7.1) and have students pick their mysteries.	**3** Have students research their historical mystery (see Handout 7.2).	**4** Have students research their historical mystery.	**5** Have students research their historical mystery.
6 Have students research their historical mystery.	**7** Have students research their historical mystery.	**8** Have students begin writing their essay.	**9** Have students continue writing their essay.	**10** Have students continue writing their essay.
11 Have students continue writing their essay.	**12** Have students complete writing their essay.	**13** Have students conduct peer reviews (see Handout 7.3).	**14** Have students complete their final draft.	

LESSON

Introduction to Historical Mysteries

Distribute Handout 7.1: Structure of the Essay and demonstrate the formatting of the project. You may use Stonehenge or another historical mystery as an example as you discuss the outline.

Tell students they will need to introduce their mystery in the introduction. For example: *Stonehenge, located in Wiltshire, England, is a megalith (Greek for great stones). It is a stone structure made up of a series of two vertical stones topped by a horizontal one. There are 40 of these stones, standing 24 or more feet high. Stonehenge is one of 50,000 megaliths in Europe. Dozens of stone rings are scattered around Great Britain alone. Some theorize this series of stone rings forms a network.*

There are many unanswered questions about Stonehenge:

- Who built Stonehenge?
- How was Stonehenge constructed considering the lack of tools?
- Why was Stonehenge built?
- What purpose does Stonehenge serve?

Tell students that there are many theories that answer these questions. The rest of the essay should discuss three theories. For example:

- **Theory 1:** *One theory is that Druid priests built Stonehenge. This idea began when John Aubrey, a 17th-century scientist, discovered what he thought were Pagan temples. Druid priests performed many religious ceremonies around Stonehenge. They were the priests of the ancient Britons, and thus they were the people who would construct temples. There are several pieces of evidence to back this theory up. For one, there have been bodies found near Stonehenge, which are believed to be sacrifices, and the Druids were into sacrifices. Druids are addicted to Magik in which the circle is very sacred, and Stonehenge is in a circular shape. Druids continue to this day to worship around Stonehenge and have been granted permission to do so by the British government. One problem with this theory is that with carbon dating it has been determined that Stonehenge was built by 1500 B.C. This is well before the Druids came to Britain. Another problem is that Druids usually hold their ceremonies in forests, not in the open as Stonehenge.*
- **Theory 2:** *Another theory is that Stonehenge was built as an astronomical device. A scientist by the name of John Hawkins linked Stonehenge to the sky, saying that it was aligned with certain celestial bodies. The evidence that supports this theory is that the sun rises precisely over the heel stone, leading some to believe it was placed there on purpose. Other stones align with the horizon as well. The summer and winter solstice were part of the alignment, marking significant risings and settings of the moon and*

sun. In addition, the narrowness between the pillars acts as a field of observation to force the eyes to see. The problem with Hawkins' theory is that in order for it to work, some stones had to be ignored while others were deemed more significant to fit in with the theory. Also, the holes between the stones were not necessarily caused by hand but by roots of tree growing through. The last problem is that if the measurements were off, even by two degrees, it could totally miss the celestial bodies.

- **Theory 3:** *A final theory is that Stonehenge is a religious or government center for another civilization. An architect, Inigo Jones, was hired by King James I and was the first person to really study Stonehenge. Jones believed it was a Roman building to the gods. Others believe Greeks or Phoenicians built it for a government center. What leads some to believe this theory is that there are many similarities to Roman architecture. Also, the Romans were the only ones with the skills to construct such a building. A dagger shape on one of the stones is like one found in Crete which adds further proof. Some objects in nearby graves show a Mediterranean influence. The major problem with this theory is similar to the first theory: the actual date of the construction of Stonehenge was before the Romans came to Britain. And if the Romans did indeed base it on their architecture, the structure is too primitive for the sophisticated Romans. Even though the dagger marking is similar to one in Crete, there are no traditional Roman engravings or inscriptions such as on other Roman-made buildings.*

After discussing three theories, students will need to conclude their essays with the theory they believe best explains their historical mystery. For example:

Theory #2 seems the most likely. There seems to be a lot of proof that there are celestial alignments with some of the structures of Stonehenge. The sunrise being directly over the heel-stone, as well as the alignment with the summer and winter solstice, leads me to believe it was used as an astronomy device. Even with the problems of the degress being a little off here and there, Stonehenge is thousands of years old. There has been a lot of shifting of the structures as well as weathering and humans messing with it. It makes sense that some of these alignments no longer apply, but probably when it was initially used they lined up perfectly.

Name: ______________________ Date: ______________

HANDOUT 7.1

Structure of the Essay

Directions: This is the basic outline of your historical mystery essay.

1. **Introduction:** Explain the historical mystery. What are the basic facts behind the mystery—the who, what, when, and where? You are introducing the topic to readers so that they can gain an understanding of the event.

2. **Theory 1:** Discuss one theory that explains the historical mystery, giving a summary of the theory and the evidence that supports it.

3. **Theory 2:** Discuss a second theory that explains the historical mystery, giving a summary of the theory and the evidence that supports it.

4. **Theory 3:** Discuss a a third theory that explains the historical mystery, giving a summary of the theory and the evidence that supports it.

5. **Conclusion:** Choose which theory you believe best explains the historical mystery and justify your reasons for choosing this theory.

Name: ______________________________ Date: ______________

HANDOUT 7.2

Research Notes

Directions: Use this graphic organizer to organize your research.

Section	Notes	Works Cited
Introduction		
Theory 1		

Name: ______________________________ Date: ______________

Handout 7.2: Research Notes, *continued*

Section	Notes	Works Cited
Theory 2		
Theory 3		
Conclusion		

Name: ______________________________ Date: ______________

HANDOUT 7.3

Peer Review

Directions: Evaluate each section of the essay using the appropriate letter grade. A = excellent, while F = not present or completely wrong.

Peer's Name: ____________________ Peer's Essay Topic: ____________________

Criteria	Grade	Comments
Introduction *Is the purpose of the paper clearly established?*	A B C D F	
Use of Evidence *Does the author use reliable examples to back up statements made?*	A B C D F	
Defense of Theory *Does the author make a sound argument in the conclusion?*	A B C D F	
Mechanics *How is the spelling, punctuation, and sentence structure?*	A B C D F	
Structure *Does the essay follow a clear five-part structure?*	A B C D F	

Name: ______________________ Date: ______________

PRODUCT RUBRIC

Greatest Historical Mysteries

Mystery:			
Overall	**Content**	**Conclusion**	**Grammar/Spelling**
Excellent (A)	◆ Student clearly determines two or more main ideas of a text and explains how they are supported by key details. ◆ Student consistently refers to details and examples in the text when drawing inferences from the text. ◆ Student consistently draws specific evidence from the informational text to support each of the paragraphs.	◆ Student clearly chooses a theory to support and explains how the author uses reasons and evidence to support particular points in a text. ◆ Student supports a point of view with reasons and information to make an argument for the choice.	◆ Essay has little to no spelling/grammar errors. ◆ Essay uses capitalization correctly consistently. ◆ Sentence structure is consistently clear, making the essay easy to read and understand.
Good (B–C)	◆ Student determines two or more main ideas of a text and explains how they are supported by key details, but there are times where the explanation is not clear. ◆ Student refers to details and examples in the text when drawing inferences from the text in most cases, but there are places where there could have been more. ◆ Student draws specific evidence from the informational text to support most of the paragraphs, but some need further evidence.	◆ Student chooses a theory to support and explains how the author uses reasons and evidence to support particular points in a text but could be clearer in explanation. ◆ Student supports a point of view with reasons and information but needs more evidence.	◆ Essay has some occasional spelling/grammar errors. ◆ Essay uses capitalization correctly but not always consistently. ◆ Sentence structure is mostly clear, making the essay easy to read and understand, but there are a few spots where it is difficult to follow.
Needs Improvement (D–F)	◆ Student does not determine two or more main ideas of a text and/or explain how they are supported by key details. ◆ Student does not refer to details and examples in the text when drawing inferences from the text. ◆ Student does not consistently draw specific evidence from the text to support each paragraph, failing to support each theory.	◆ Student does not choose a theory to support and/or does not explain how the author uses reasons and evidence to support particular points in a text. ◆ Student does not support a point of view with reasons and information, leaving the argument unconvincing.	◆ Essay has many spelling/grammar errors, making it difficult to read. ◆ Essay does not use capitalization correctly consistently. ◆ Sentence structure is not clear, making the essay difficult to read and understand.

8 Research Paper

One way to look at a research paper is as an expanded essay. Essentially, it follows the same structure: introduction of thesis, evidence, and conclusion. The big difference is that students are also responsible for conducting independent research. For an essay, the teacher often provides the background information or data for a student to be able to answer the question presented in an essay format. The students are merely synthesizing what they have learned from the teacher and communicating how it fits into the essay. The essay can be written on the spot and is a culmination of what has been taught. A research paper, on the other hand, has the students acquiring the information for themselves by using various sources, including books, the Internet, or interviews. The writing aspect is the last thing the student will be doing. There is the process of finding, evaluating, and organizing the information. Finally, the student must properly cite sources.

What It Looks Like

The key to a good research paper is providing an outline for students to follow. The outline can be very basic or it can be detailed depending on the level of the student. The outline should walk students through what is expected in the paper. Students should be able to use this as a blueprint to construct their research paper.

It is important for students to understand there is a structure to a research paper and that the outline is the backbone around which they will build the research. Once they understand this and have a solid outline, the creation of the paper becomes a matter of building it around the outline. This will make the writing of all future research papers easier.

What Do You Want to Be When You Grow Up?

In this project, students will research a career they are interested in pursuing. They will research the education and training that goes into the job, how much someone in the field makes, and how difficult it is to get into the career. They will then write a paper that shows in detail what someone in this career would have to do to become qualified. This should include their reasons for wanting to pursue the career, as well as quotes from people who are currently in this career.

Connections to CCSS

- RI.3.1
- RI.3.7
- RI.3.9
- RI.4.1
- RI.4.7
- RI.4.9
- RI.5.1
- RI.5.7
- RI.5.9
- W.3.2
- W.3.7
- W.3.10
- W.4.2
- W.4.7
- W.4.10
- W.5.2
- W.5.7
- W.5.10

Materials

- Project Outline: What Do You Want to Be When You Grow Up? (student copies)
- Suggested Timeline
- Lesson: Conducting Research
- Handout 8.1: Internet Scavenger Hunt (student copies)
- Handout 8.2: Researching Your Topic (student copies)
- Product Rubric (student copies)

Name: ______________________ Date: ______________

PROJECT OUTLINE

What Do You Want to Be When You Grow Up?

Directions: You will research a career you are interested in pursuing. You will research the education and training that goes into the job, how much someone in the field makes, and how difficult it is to get into the career.

You will then write a paper that shows in detail what someone in this career would have to do to become qualified. This should include your reasons for wanting to pursue the career, as well as quotes from people who are currently in this career.

There should be four sections to your paper:

- Introduction
  - What is the career you are interested in?
  - How did you become interested in it?
  - Why do you want to do this as a career?

- Career opportunities
  - What exactly would someone do in the career you are interested in?
  - What are the opportunities in this field you have chosen?
  - Are jobs plentiful or is there a hierarchy in the job field that you have to work your way up?
  - Are there many people doing this job or are there only a few select?
  - Is there an organization for your field to turn to for support, like a union or guild?

- Training for your profession
  - What does one have to do to be qualified to be in your profession?
  - Is there special training or school to be in your profession? What exactly does this entail?

- Conclusion
  - Now that you have researched it, are you still interested in this career?
  - Is this career what you expected it would be?
  - Do you think pursuing this career will be a difficult or easy task and why?
  - What are your career goals with this profession?

SUGGESTED TIMELINE

DAY **1** Introduce the project and have students take an online career prognosticator.	**2** Conduct Lesson: Conducting Research (see Handout 8.1, Handout 8.2).	**3** Have students conduct research on their career.	**4** Have students conduct research on their career.	**5** Have students conduct research on their career.
6 Have students conduct research on their career.	**7** Students need to begin the rough draft of their career paper.	**8** Students need to continue the rough draft of their career paper.	**9** Students need to continue the rough draft of their career paper.	**10** Students need to finish the rough draft of their career paper.
11 Have students revise their rough draft.	**12** Students need to begin the final draft of their career paper.	**13** Students need to continue the final draft of their career paper.	**14** Students need to continue the final draft of their career paper.	**15** Students need to finish the final draft of their career paper.

LESSON

Conducting Research

Tell students that they can find almost anything on the Internet, which means they will always have to go through a lot of information that might not be relevant to their topic.

There are various search engines to help them find information, such as:

- Google (http://www.google.com),
- Yahoo (http://www.yahoo.com), and
- Bing (http://www.bing.com).

When they search, they will want to:

- be as specific as possible without being too specific (e.g., too general = "airplanes," too specific = "paper airplanes with cool decals");
- narrow their search without eliminating sites because they do not contain the exact wording; and
- not just use the first website they encounter (i.e., just because it comes up in a search does not mean it is what they are looking for).

Distribute Handout 8.1: Internet Scavenger Hunt. Tell students to imagine they are writing a report about baseball. If they Google the term "baseball," they retrieve more than 450,000,000 results. That's more than anyone can possibly go through. How do they refine their search? The scavenger hunt will show them how.

Have students select their research topics and distribute Handout 8.2: Researching Your Topic.

Name: ______________________________ Date: ______________

HANDOUT 8.1

Internet Scavenger Hunt

Directions: Use a search engine to answer the following questions.

1. How many hits do you get when you put in the search term "baseball"?

2. How many hits do you receive when you refine your search to "baseball rules"?

3. How many hits do you receive when you refine your search to "baseball rules for kids"?

4. If you are trying to find out how many feet between bases, what key term could you use to refine your search even more?

5. Using one of the three search engines, determine who has the record for most career homeruns in Major League Baseball.

Name: ______________________________ Date: ______________

Handout 8.1: Internet Scavenger Hunt, *continued*

6. How many teams are there currently in Major League Baseball?

7. What is the definition of a "balk"?

8. Who is often falsely credited with inventing baseball?

9. Go to http://www.mlb.com. Under "Teams" in the top menu, go to "Chicago Cubs." Then under "Roster," go to "Depth Chart." Who is the top name for the second base position?

10. Go to the Baseball Hall of Fame at http://www.baseballhall.org. Search for "Roberto Clemente" to see what year he was elected to the Hall of Fame.

Name: ______________________________ Date: ______________

HANDOUT 8.2

Researching Your Topic

Directions: When you are conducting research you should consider the following five steps.

Step 1: Construct Research Questions

Write specific questions. Doing so will help you narrow your topic and determine exactly what information you need. Sample questions:

- Who were the best baseball players?
- How did baseball get started?
- What are some of the rules of baseball?
- How does one become a professional baseball player?
- Who holds many of the records in baseball?
- How many baseball teams are there currently?

Step 2: Figure Out Possible Sources of Information

Before going online, try to identify any sources that might have information on your topic. For example, you might list:

- National Baseball Hall of Fame
- Society for American Baseball Research
- Anything affiliated with Major League Baseball
- PBS/ESPN/MLB (might have documentaries on famous baseball players or events or have information or interactive explorations on their websites)

Step 3: Identify Keywords

Review the questions and sources you brainstormed in Steps 1–2, and circle the keywords. What is it specifically you want to find? Use this to refine your search.

Name: ______________________________ Date: ______________

Handout 8.2: Researching Your Topic, *continued*

Step 4: Get Ready to Search

You are finally ready to choose a tool(s) and begin your search. Depending on the time you have and your own personal preference, you can start with a search engine or a specific site of your own choice.

If you are using a search engine, you will want to use the keywords you identified in Step 3 to develop your search query. The trick is to try several combinations of keywords, using terms from all three columns in your keyword chart. Remember—there's no one *right* way to conduct research online. Just be sure to start with a strategy and experiment with different search tools to get the best results.

Step 5: Finding Easy-To-Understand, School-Appropriate Sites

Adding a simple suffix to your search may result in more student-appropriate, student-friendly results. For instance, refine your search to add the following:

- . . . for kids
- . . . for students
- . . . for children
- . . . for school

These will make the hits you receive from your search more age appropriate and easier to understand because you will be the audience they are written for.

Name: ______________________________ Date: ________________

PRODUCT RUBRIC

What Do You Want to Be When You Grow Up?

Career:			
Overall	**Content**	**Paper**	**Research**
Excellent (A)	• Paper follows the outline clearly. • Student gives plenty of examples to back up statements. • Student provides much detail, explaining concepts and ideas fully.	• Paper has little to no spelling/grammar errors. • Paper is typed in the correct format. • Paper uses a sentence structure that makes the paragraphs flow and easy to read.	• Research is consistently put into student's own words, paraphrasing information. • Student uses specific facts and data where necessary, giving the reader a clear picture. • Student uses several quotes from people practicing this career to convey information and make points.
Good (B–C)	• Paper follows the outline but is hard to follow at times. • Student gives examples to back up statements but not consistently. • Student provides detail, explaining concepts and ideas, but could be clearer.	• Paper has occasional spelling/grammar errors, making more than a handful of mistakes. • Paper is typed but not always in the correct format. • Paper mostly uses a sentence structure that makes the paragraphs flow and easy to read but has the occasional awkward sentence that causes confusion.	• Research is paraphrased, but student occasionally uses terms and phrases not their own. • Student uses facts and data, but they may not be very specific or used in every place they are needed. • Student uses a couple of quotes from people practicing this career to convey information and make points but could use more.

Name: ______________________ Date: ______________

Project Rubric: What Do You Want to Be When You Grow Up?, *continued*

Overall	Content	Paper	Research
Needs Improvement (D–F)	• Paper does not follow the outline, causing the reader confusion about what is being discussed at any given time because parts are left out. • Student provides little to no examples to back up statements made in the paper. • Student does not provide much detail, leaving the reader confused about what is being discussed.	• Paper has many spelling/grammar errors, making it difficult to read the paper at times. • Paper is typed in a sloppy manner, making it difficult to read. • Paper has a sloppy sentence structure that makes the paragraphs difficult to follow and makes it unclear what is being written about.	• Research is many times not put into student's own words, using terms and phrases not his or her own. • Student does not use facts and data where necessary, leaving the reader with more questions than answers. • Student uses little to no quotes from people practicing this career to convey information and make points.

9 Journal/ Student Log

Journals and student logs allow for a more informal style of writing. Although it is important for students to be able to write a proper essay, it is also important to give students the opportunity to be creative and not be constrained by the structure of an essay. Journals and student logs allow students to explore ideas without being tied to an essay format. The format need not even include complete sentences. Students can draw, write poetry, make lists, write letters from the perspective of another person, draw charts, or use any other form of expression.

Journals also do not need to be exclusive to language arts class. Students can journal in science, social studies, math, and even gym class. Journals show the progression of learning. Students can go back and see how much they have learned and what route they took to get there.

What It Looks Like

The nice thing about journal entries is that unlike an essay or research paper, which has a clear structure, there is more flexibility to look like whatever the teacher or student wishes for it to be. Journal entries usually start with a prompt. Writing prompts using higher level language allow for higher level thinking. It is important not to encourage lower level journal entries by assigning lower level prompts. Using key words from Bloom's taxonomy to do this will help in the writing of these higher level prompts (Sedita, 2012).

Everybody Has One Good Book in Them, But Do Any Have Two?

In this project, students will look at works by the same author. They will create a journal that compares three or more works by the same author, looking at the similarities and differences in them. They will need to divide each book into three sections, reading a section a week.

Connections to CCSS

- RL.3.1
- RL.3.2
- RL.3.3
- RL.3.9
- RL.4.1
- RL.4.2
- RL.4.3
- RL.4.9
- RL.5.1
- RL.5.2
- RL.5.3
- RL.5.9
- RI.3.5
- RI.4.5
- RI.5.5
- W.3.2
- W.3.4
- W.4.2
- W.4.4
- W.5.2
- W.5.5

Note. This project can be adjusted to only compare two books or as many as four books depending on the level of your students as readers.

Materials

- Project Outline: Everybody Has One Good Book in Them, But Do Any Have Two? (student copies)
- Suggested Timeline
- Handout 9.1: Journal Prompts (student copies)
- Product Rubric (student copies)

Name: ______________________ Date: ______________

PROJECT OUTLINE

Everybody Has One Good Book in Them, But Do Any Have Two?

Directions: You will look at works by the same author. You might want to compare two or three of the Diary of a Wimpy Kid books by Jeff Kinney, or look at Judy Blume's *Superfudge* compared to *Tales of a Fourth Grade Nothing* compared to *Otherwise Known as Sheila the Great*.

You will create a journal that compares three or more works by the same author, looking at the similarities and differences in them. You will need to divide each book into three sections, reading a section a week. For example, if the book is 150 pages long, you will read 50 pages a week. For each section you will have two journal entries to complete.

Guidelines For Journal Entries

1. Write legibly.
2. Spelling and grammar are not as big of a concern as communicating clearly and effectively.
3. Refer to specific instances in the text as much as possible (can even include page numbers).
4. Each journal entry should be at least a page long.
5. Always explain why you made the decision you made, as well as what it was.
6. Share your feelings or opinions, but make sure you justify them with an explanation.
7. Be willing to try new things.

SUGGESTED TIMELINE

WEEK
1 Introduce the project—have students choose the author they want to use for the project.
2 Students should start the first book and write Journal Entries 1 and 2.
3 Students should continue the first book and write Journal Entries 3 and 4.
4 Students should finish the first book and write Journal Entries 5 and 6.
6 Students should start the second book and write Journal Entries 7 and 8.
7 Students should continue the second book and write Journal Entries 9 and 10.
8 Students should finish the second book and write Journal Entries 11 and 12.
9 Students should start the third book and write Journal Entries 13 and 14.
10 Students should continue the third book and write Journal Entries 15 and 16.
11 Students should finish the third book and write Journal Entries 17 and 18.
12 Students should work on their analysis of the three books, drawing comparisons and contrasts in Journal Entries 19 and 20.

Name: ______________________________ Date: ________________

HANDOUT 9.1

Journal Prompts

Directions: You should use the following prompts as guidance in writing your journal entries. Although the journals do not need to be formal, they do need to provide plenty of detail and examples so that the reader can see where you are coming from.

Section 1: Book Analysis

- **Entry 1:** From whose perspective is the book told? Why do you think the author chose this person? Would you have chosen this person or another character?
- **Entry 2**: What is the primary setting of the book? What evidence from the text supports this? Why do you think the author chose this setting? Do you think a different setting would have been more effective or interesting? Why or why not?
- **Entry 3:** Compare and contrast two or more characters, settings, or events in your book, drawing on specific details in the text.
- **Entry 4:** How do characters in the story respond to challenges? What do you think this reveals about who they are? What evidence from the text can you provide to back this up?
- **Entry 5:** How would you describe the theme of the book? What examples from the text lead you to believe this?
- **Entry 6:** Write a review of the book. In this review, you must summarize the story and provide an opinion on whether you liked the book or not. Make sure to use specific examples from the book to support your decisions.

Repeat entries 1–6 for the second and third books.

Section 2: Analysis of Series

- **Entry 19:** Compare and contrast the overall structure of events, ideas, concepts, or information in the texts.
- **Entry 20:** Using the notes from your journal entries, compare and contrast the themes, settings, and plots of all three stories.

Name: ______________________ Date: ______________

PRODUCT RUBRIC

Everybody Has One Good Book in Them, But Do Any Have Two?

Overall	Clarity of Writing	Analysis	Journal
Excellent (A)	◆ Student produces clear and coherent writing in which the development and organization are easy to follow. ◆ Journal consistently conveys ideas and information clearly by providing details and examples to illustrate points.	◆ Journal compares and contrasts the structure of events, ideas, concepts, or information, citing several specific examples from the text. ◆ Journal compares and contrasts the themes, settings, and plots of stories using many specific textual examples.	◆ There are 20 journal entries. ◆ Journal entries consistently follow the guidelines. ◆ Journal is organized so specific entries can be easily located.
Good (B–C)	◆ Student produces clear and coherent writing in which the development and organization are easy to follow in most entries. ◆ Journal conveys ideas and information by providing details and examples to illustrate most points but not all.	◆ Journal compares and contrasts the overall structure of events, ideas, concepts, or information, almost always citing examples from the text. ◆ Journal compares and contrasts the themes, settings, and plots of stories, almost always using textual examples.	◆ There are 16–19 journal entries. ◆ Journal entries follow the guidelines for the most part. ◆ Journal is organized so that specific entries can be located, but a few entries are out of order.
Needs Improvement (D–F)	◆ Student does not produce clear and coherent writing in which the development and organization are easy to follow. ◆ Journal does not often convey ideas and information clearly due to lack of details and examples to illustrate points.	◆ Journal does not compare and contrast the overall structure of events, ideas, concepts, or information, or does not cite specific examples from the text. ◆ Journal does not compare and contrast the themes, settings, and plots of stories, or does not use specific textual examples.	◆ There are 15 or fewer journal entries. ◆ Journal entries do not follow the guidelines. ◆ Journal is unorganized to the point where the reader has to search for entries or cannot locate them all.

10 Portfolio

A student portfolio is a collection of materials that represents what a student learned. It may be something as simple as a folder containing the student's best work, along with the student's evaluation of this work. It may also be articles or work from other sources that the student has commented or reflected on. The length of the portfolio is determined by the teacher. The portfolio could be a snapshot of what the student learned during a brief one-week project, or it can be an ongoing evolution of how that student has improved over the course of an entire year. For instance, the first part of a portfolio might contain an essay the student wrote on the first day of class. The remaining content of the portfolio might show work 6 weeks in, 12 weeks in, or at the semester break. What can be seen throughout this process is how the student has improved and acquired new skills or knowledge. Conceivably, a portfolio could track the student's progress for an entire year and even longer. The assessment of a portfolio comes more from the student commentary than it does from the pieces she selected as part of the portfolio. This commentary can be as informal as a student jotting down an observation from a highlighted piece of text to a formal essay that sums up the entire project or semester. Either one of these can be used in the classroom as a performance-based assessment.

What It Looks Like

According to Melissa Kelly (2014), there are three main factors that go into the development of a student portfolio assessment:

> First, you must decide the purpose of your portfolio. For example, the portfolios might be used to show student growth, to identify weak spots in student work, and/or to evaluate your own teaching methods.
>
> After deciding the purpose of the portfolio, you will need to determine how you are going to grade it. In other words, what would a student need in her portfolio for it to be considered a success and for her to earn a passing grade?
>
> What should be included in the portfolio? Are you going to have students put of all of their work or only certain assignments? Who gets to choose? (para. 9)

Funerary

In the poem anthology *Spoon River*, Edgar Lee Masters paints a portrait of the town of Spoon River through the headstones in its cemetery. What do the headstones in your town cemetery say about your town? What sort of history is captured on these slabs of granite?

In this project, students will select three headstones at a local cemetery that they find interesting. They will investigate the history behind one of the headstones, including the time span of the person's life and major events that were going on in the world during that time. They will also write a series of poems covering the life of the individuals their headstones represent—from their childhood to adulthood. They will collect all of this in a portfolio.

Connections to CCSS

- RL.3.5
- RL.4.5
- RL.5.5
- RL.5.7
- RI.5.7
- RI.5.10

Materials

- Project Outline: Funerary (student copies)
- Suggested Timeline
- Lesson: Poetry Analysis
- Handout 10.1: Headstone History (student copies)
- Handout 10.2: Scientific Innovations (student copies)
- Handout 10.3: Edgar Lee Masters Poems (student copies)
- Handout 10.4: Poetry Analysis (student copies)
- Handout 10.5: Writing a Masters-Style Poem (student copies)
- Product Rubric (student copies)

Name: ______________________________ Date: ______________

PROJECT OUTLINE

Funerary

Directions: In the poem anthology *Spoon River*, Edgar Lee Masters paints a portrait of the town of Spoon River through the headstones in its cemetery. What do the headstones in your town cemetery say about your town? What sort of history is captured on these slabs of granite?

You will select three headstones at a local cemetery that you find interesting. You will investigate the history behind one of the headstones, including the time span of the person's life and major events that were going on in the world during that time. You will also write a series of poems covering the life of the individuals your headstones represent—from their childhood to adulthood. You will collect all of this in a portfolio.

Parts of the Portfolio

1. **Section 1: Headstones.** Select three headstones, one with a saying and one with a visual.
2. **Section 2: History.** Research five topics from the time period of one of your headstones.
3. **Section 3: Science.** Research three scientific innovations from the time period of your headstone and the long-term effects.
4. **Section 4: Language Arts.** Analyze three Masters Poems.
5. **Section 5:Writing.** Create three poems in the style of Masters based on your headstones.

Selecting Headstones

To select your headstones, you will either go on a class field trip to a local cemetery, have a parent take you to a cemetery, or locate three headstones on the Internet.

1. Identify three headstones from 1980 or before.
2. One must have text (i.e., poem or saying) to accompany it.
3. One must have a distinctive visual on the headstone.
4. One must span at least 20 years from birth to death.
5. You can create rubbings of the headstones.

SUGGESTED TIMELINE

DAY				
1 Introduce the project.	**2** Have students choose three headstones they would like to study. If possible, take a field trip to a local cemetery with older headstones.	**3** Have students record the headstones they chose and record them in their portfolios.	**4** Have students begin to research the time period of one of their headstones (see Handout 10.1).	**5** Have students continue to research the time period of one of their headstones.
6 Have students continue to research the time period of one of their headstones.	**7** Have students continue to research the time period of one of their headstones.	**8** Have students finish researching the time period of one of their headstones, collecting responses in their portfolio.	**9** Have students research three scientific innovations during the time period of one of their headstones (see Handout 10.2).	**10** Have students research three scientific innovations during the time period of their headstone.
11 Have students research three scientific innovations during the time period of their headstone.	**12** Have students record three scientific innovations during the time period of their headstone and their significance in their portfolio.	**13** Conduct Lesson: Poetry Analysis (see Handout 10.3 and Handout 10.4).	**14** Conduct a class discussion about the poem analysis.	**15** Conduct a class discussion about the poem analysis.

Suggested Timeline, *continued*

DAY				
16 Have students choose three of their own Masters poems to analyze in their portfolio.	**17** Have students analyze their first Masters poem.	**18** Have students analyze their second Masters poem.	**19** Have students analyze their third Masters poem.	**20** Have students create a drawing or visual for poems they analyzed.
21 Discuss patterns in Masters's poems (see Handout 10.5).	**22** Have students write a practice poem about themselves in the style of Masters.	**23** Have students write a poem based on Headstone 1.	**24** Have students write a poem based on Headstone 2.	**25** Have students write a poem based on Headstone 3.

LESSON

Poetry Analysis

Distribute Handout 10.3: Edgar Lee Masters Poems and three copies of Handout 10.4: Poetry Analysis to each student, allowing students time to complete the questions. The following analysis will assist with a class discussion about the poems. Sample responses are provided, although student answers may vary, provided they can justify their responses.

Rev. Abner Peet Analysis

1. **What is the name of the person the poem is about?** *Rev. Abner Peet.*

2. **Summarize what the poem is about.** *After Rev. Peet died, they decided to sell his household items to the highest bidder at the town square. Rev. Peet seemed flattered at first that his flock was buying the items in memorial for him but then was offended when his sermons were purchased by the town bar owner and then burned for waste paper.*

3. **What does the poem tell us about this person? What evidence in the poem points to this?** *It seems as though Reverend Peet is a little full of himself in that he is flattered when people are buying his possessions because he believes it means that he was beloved by the people and they want to own something that once belonged to him. Then when he finds out that Burchard the grog-keeper was simply buying his sermons to use as waste paper in the fire, he is offended that his lifetime of work is being used in this manner. It makes one wonder if maybe others bought his possessions not because they reminded them of him but because they had a practical use for them.*

4. **How do you feel this person fit into the town of Spoon River? What leads you to believe this?** *I believed Reverend Peet might have thought more of himself than the town thought of him. The fact that they sold all of his possessions after his death in the town square could show that he was not that important. And the fact that his sermons, the representation of a lifetime of work toward the town, were used as waste paper for the fire might show that they did not think that highly of him.*

5. **Include a drawing or visual that adds to the meaning, tone, or beauty of the text.**

6. **Why did you choose this visual and what does it add to our understanding of this person?** *I chose this golden cross because Rev. Peet was a man of God, which the cross represents. But I chose a very gaudy, ornamental cross to show his vanity and how he thought a lot of himself.*

Judge Somers Analysis

1. **What is the name of the person the poem is about?** *Judge Somers.*

2. **Summarize what the poem is about.** *Judge Somers thought himself to be an intelligent lawyer who made the greatest speech the courthouse ever heard. And yet when he was buried he was put in an unmarked grave and has been forgotten about, while the town drunkard has a marble block topped by an urn.*

3. **What does the poem tell us about this person? What evidence in the poem points to this?** *Judge Somers definitely seems a bit bitter that the town drunk is more remembered than he is. He compares this town drunkard to a flowering weed that the town has sown while he has been forgotten. He also thinks very highly of his skills as a lawyer, bragging that he gave the greatest speech the courthouse has ever heard and how he wrote a brief that won the praise of Justice Breese.*

4. **How do you feel this person fit into the town of Spoon River? What leads you to believe this?** *Because he has been forgotten, I do not think the town thought he was as important as he thought himself. Although he brags about being such a great lawyer, he was buried in an unmarked grave, usually a sign of not being that important.*

5. **Include a drawing or visual that adds to the meaning, tone, or beauty of the text.**

6. **Why did you choose this visual and what does it add to our understanding of this person?** *I chose a blank headstone because the people of Spoon River have forgotten about Judge Somers. The fact that there are absolutely no markings on the headstones show that Judge Somers did not leave any markings on the memories of the townspeople.*

Lydia Puckett Analysis

1. **What is the name of the person the poem is about?** *Lydia Puckett.*

2. **Summarize what the poem is about.** *Most of the story is about how Knowlt Hoheimer ran away to war and the reasons he did this. Most people think he did this because he was caught stealing hogs and Justice Arnett had issued a warrant for his arrest, but Lydia reveals that she had been dating Knowlt but then went with another boy and Knowlt found out. She told him never to cross her path again, so then he stole the hogs and ran off to war.*

3. **What does the poem tell us about this person? What evidence in the poem points to this?** *What this poem tells us about Lydia is that she seems to feel guilty that she was the cause of Knowlt Hoheimer running off to war. She says "Back of every soldier is a woman," possibly meaning that every person willing to fight in a war does so because of a woman. Because she takes the blame for his running off, she obviously feels bad for causing that because she easily could have blamed it on the hog stealing like most people in the town thought.*

4. **How do you feel this person fit into the town of Spoon River? What leads you to believe this?** *Obviously she was really popular with the boys in the town because she had not one but two boyfriends in Knowlt and Lucius Atherton. Since everyone thinks that Knowlt ran off because he stole the pigs, it doesn't seem the town blames her for it, only that her own guilt causes her to confess.*

5. **Include a drawing or visual that adds to the meaning, tone, or beauty of the text.**

6. **Why did you choose this visual and what does it add to our understanding of this person?** *I chose two rifles and a broken heart because the guns represent Knowlt going off to war, he having a rifle, and his enemy having a rifle. The broken heart in the middle of them shows that it was his broken heart caused by Lydia Puckett that made him to go off and volunteer for the war.*

Name: ______________________________ Date: ______________

HANDOUT 10.1

Headstone History

Directions: Choose five of the following eight topics to research and write about one of your headstones, citing your sources.

1. Create a timeline that spans the length of years on your headstone. List 10 important events that happened during this span and their significance.
2. Include a map of the world during the time period of your headstone as well as a current map of the world. What are the differences and similarities in them?
3. Compare the prices of five things found at a grocery store during the time period of your headstone and now.
4. What was a popular movie/song/book during that time and a popular movie/song/book now? What do these indicate about the society in which they were made?
5. Who was president during this time period and how are his leadership abilities/policies/concerns different than the current president's?
6. What was a common job for women during the time of your headstone? Has that changed from what a common job for women currently would be?
7. How have schools changed from the time period of your headstone to the way they currently operate?
8. What has changed about the town you live in from the time of your headstone compared to now?

Name: ______________________________ Date: ______________

Handout 10.1: Headstone History, *continued*

How to Create Works Cited

When looking up information on the Internet or in a book, it is important to give credit to the source. One way to do this is by creating a works cited page. The following is one way you could format citations.

Citing an Online Encyclopedia:
Author (if known). "Title of article." *Name of encyclopedia*. Name of publisher, date of publication (if available). Date of your visit. Name of the online service you used.

For example:
"Abraham Lincoln." *Wikipedia: The Free Encyclopedia*. 2016. Web. 1 May 2016.

Citing a Webpage:
Author (if known). "Title of article." *Title of website*. Date of your visit. URL.

For example:
Kelly, Martin. "Abraham Lincoln—16th President of the United States." *About Education*. 1 May 2016. http://americanhistory.about.com/od/abrahamlincoln/p/plincoln.htm

Name: ______________________________ Date: ______________

HANDOUT 10.2

Scientific Innovations

Scientific Innovation 1

1. What is a major scientific innovation during this time period and when did it take place?

2. How did this scientific innovation have an impact on society at the time?

3. What is the long-term significance of this scientific innovation on today's world?

Scientific Innovation 2

1. What is a major scientific innovation during this time period and when did it take place?

Name: ______________________________ Date: ______________

Handout 10.2: Scientific Innovations, *continued*

2. How did this scientific innovation have an impact on society at the time?

3. What is the long-term significance of this scientific innovation on today's world?

Scientific Innovation 3

1. What is a major scientific innovation during this time period and when did it take place?

2. How did this scientific innovation have an impact on society at the time?

3. What is the long-term significance of this scientific innovation on today's world?

Name: ______________________ Date: ______________

HANDOUT 10.3

Edgar Lee Masters Poems

Rev. Abner Peet

I had no objection at all
To selling my household effects at auction
On the village square.
It gave my beloved flock the chance
To get something which had belonged to me
For a memorial.
But that trunk which was struck off
To Burchard, the grog-keeper!
Did you know it contained the manuscripts
Of a lifetime of sermons?
And he burned them as waste paper.

Judge Somers

How does it happen, tell me,
That I who was most erudite of lawyers,
Who knew Blackstone and Coke
Almost by heart, who made the greatest speech
The court-house ever heard, and wrote
A brief that won the praise of Justice Breese
How does it happen, tell me,
That I lie here unmarked, forgotten,
While Chase Henry, the town drunkard,
Has a marble block, topped by an urn
Wherein Nature, in a mood ironical,
Has sown a flowering weed?

Name: ____________________ Date: ____________

Handout 10.3: Edgar Lee Masters Poems, *continued*

Lydia Puckett

Knowlt Hoheimer ran away to the war
The day before Curl Trenary
Swore out a warrant through Justice Arnett
For stealing hogs.
But that's not the reason he turned a soldier.
He caught me running with Lucius Atherton.
We quarreled and I told him never again
To cross my path.
Then he stole the hogs and went to the war -
Back of every soldier is a woman.

Name: ______________________ Date: ______________

HANDOUT 10.4

Poem Analysis

Directions: Use these prompts to analyze the poems of Edgar Lee Masters.

1. What is the name of the person the poem is about?

2. Summarize what the poem is about.

3. What does the poem tell us about this person? What evidence in the poem points to this?

4. How do you feel this person fit into the town of Spoon River? What leads you to believe this?

5. Include a drawing or visual that adds to the meaning, tone, or beauty of the text

6. Why did you choose this visual and what does it add to our understanding of this person?

Name: ______________________________ Date: ______________

HANDOUT 10.5

Writing a Masters-Style Poem

Directions: Use the following tips to write three Edgar Lee Masters-style poems about your headstones and a 15-line poem about yourself. What would you share from your life?

How to Write a Poem in the Style of Masters

- Anywhere from 10–20 lines long (never more than a page)
- Doesn't rhyme (free verse)
- Each line is usually one sentence, sometimes as short as a few words, sometimes two sentences
- Written from the perspective of the person telling the story (first person)
- Poems reveal facts about the characters that tells a story
- Are realistic
- Usually indicates how they died

Name: ____________________ Date: ____________________

PRODUCT RUBRIC

Funerary Project

Overall	Section 1 Headstones	Section 2 History	Section 3 Science	Section 4 Language Arts	Section 5 Writing
Excellent (A)	◆ Portfolio has three headstones from before 1980. ◆ One headstone has a meaningful inscription. ◆ One headstone has a meaningful visual.	◆ Student answers five of the questions with much detail and examples. ◆ Information is from very reliable sources, which are cited.	◆ Student explains in detail three scientific innovations from the time period. ◆ Student makes a convincing argument for the long-term effects of this innovation.	◆ Student analyzes three Masters poems with much detail and examples. ◆ Analyses include drawings or visuals that add to the meaning, tone, or beauty of the texts and are clearly explained.	◆ Student writes three poems that represent the headstones with much detail. ◆ Poems imitate the style of Masters' poems, telling a story of each person.
Good (B–C)	◆ Portfolio has three headstones but one after 1980. ◆ One headstone has an inscription but not particularly meaningful. ◆ One headstone has a visual but not very meaningful.	◆ Student answers five of the questions but not always with much detail and examples. ◆ Information is usually from very reliable sources but not all.	◆ Student explains three scientific innovations from the time period but not always with enough detail. ◆ Student makes an argument for the long-term effects of the innovations but needs to be more convincing.	◆ Student analyzes three of Masters' poems but needs to have more detail and/or examples in places. ◆ Analyses include drawings or visuals that add to the meaning, tone, or beauty of the text but are not clearly explained.	◆ Student writes three poems that represent the headstones studied but lack detail. ◆ Most of the poems imitate the style of Masters' poems, telling a story of each person, but not all three.

Name: ______________________ Date: ______________

Project Rubric: Funerary Project, *continued*

Overall	Section 1 Headstones	Section 2 History	Section 3 Science	Section 4 Language Arts	Section 5 Writing
Needs Improvement (D–F)	◆ Portfolio has two or fewer headstones or several after 1980. ◆ There isn't one with an inscription. ◆ There isn't one with a visual.	◆ Student answers four or fewer of the questions. ◆ Information is not from very reliable sources or there are no citations.	◆ Student explains two or fewer scientific innovations from the time period. ◆ Student does not really make an argument for the long-term effects of each innovation.	◆ Student analyzes two or fewer of Masters' poems. ◆ Student either does not include drawings or includes one that does not add to the meaning, tone, or beauty of the text.	◆ Student writes two or fewer poems that represent the headstones studied. ◆ Poems do not imitate the style of Masters' poems, failing to tell a story of each person.

REFERENCES

Bastiaens, T. J., & Martens, R. L. (2000). Conditions for web-based learning with real events. In B. Abbey (Ed.), *Instructional and cognitive impacts of web-based education* (pp. 1–31). Hershey, PA: Idea Group Publishing.

Brydon, S. R., & Scott, M. D. (2000). *Between one and many: The art and science of public speaking* (3rd ed.). Mountain View, CA: Mayfield.

Dunn, R., Dunn, K., & Price, G. E. (1984). *Learning style inventory.* Lawrence, KS: Price Systems.

Grant, M. M., & Branch, R. M. (2005). Project-based learning in middle school: Tracing abilities through the artifacts of learning. *Journal of Research on Technology in Education, 38,* 65–98.

Horton, R. M., Hedetniemi, T., Wiegert, E., & Wagner, J. R. (2006). Integrating curriculum through themes. *Mathematics Teaching in the Middle School, 11,* 408–414.

Johnsen-Harris, M. A. (1983). Surviving the budget crunch from an independent school perspective. *Roeper Review, 6,* 79–81.

Johnston, D. E. (2004). Measurement, scale, and theater arts. *Mathematics Teaching in the Middle School, 9,* 412–417.

Jones, G., & Kalinowski, K. (2007). Touring Mars online, real-time, in 3-D, for math and science educators and students. *Journal of Computers in Mathematics and Science Teaching, 26,* 123–136.

Kelly, M. (2014). *Student portfolios: Getting started with student portfolios.* Retrieved from http://712educators.about.com/od/portfolios/a/portfolios.htm

Kingsley, R. F. (1986). "Digging" for understanding and significance: A high school enrichment model. *Roeper Review, 9,* 37–38.

Ljung, E. J., & Blackwell, M. (1996). Project OMEGA: A winning approach for at-risk teens. *Illinois School Research and Development Journal, 33*(1), 15–17.

McMiller, T., Lee, T., Saroop, R., Green, T., & Johnson, C. M. (2006). Middle/high school students in the research laboratory: A summer internship program emphasizing the interdisciplinary nature of biology. *Biochemistry and Molecular Biology Education, 34,* 88–93.

Peterson, M. (1997). Skills to enhance problem-based learning. *Medical Education Online, 2*(3). Retrieved from http://med-ed-online.net/index.php/meo/article/view/4289

Ryan. (2013). *Why is public speaking important? 11 solid reasons why public speaking is important in your life*. Retrieved from http://publicspeaking-power.com/why-is-public-speaking-important

Renzulli, J. S., Smith, L. H., & Reis, S. M. (1982). Curriculum compacting: An essential strategy for working with gifted students. *The Elementary School Journal, 82,* 185–194.

Scholastic. (n.d.). *Tips from the insiders: How to write a political speech.* Retrieved from http://www.scholastic.com/teachers/article/tips-insiders-how-write-political-speech

Sedita, J. (2012). *The key comprehension routine: Grades 4–12* (2nd ed.). Rowley, MA: Keys to Literacy.

Stanley, T. (2011). *Project-based learning for gifted students: A handbook for the 21st-century classroom*. Waco, TX: Prufrock Press.

Stanley, T. (2014). *Performance-based assessment for 21st-century skills.* Waco, TX: Prufrock Press.

Stewart, E. D. (1981). Learning styles among gifted/talented students: Instructional technique preferences. *Exceptional Children, 48,* 134–138.

Stoof, A., Martens, R. L., Van Merriënboer, J. J. G., & Bastiaens, T. J. (2002). The boundary approach of competence: A constructivist aid for understanding and using the concept of competence. *Human Resource Development Review, 1*(3), 345–365.

Toolin, R. E. (2004). Striking a balance between innovation and standards: A study of teachers implementing project-based approaches to teaching science. *Journal of Science Education and Technology, 13,* 179–187.

Trilling, B., & Fadel, C. (2009). *21st-century skills: Learning for life in our times*. Hoboken, NJ: Jossey-Bass.

Wagner, T. (2014). *The global achievement gap: Why even our best schools don't teach the new survival skills our children need—and what we can do about it*. New York, NY: Basics Books.

Whitener, E. M. (1989). A meta-analytic review of the effect of learning on the interaction between prior achievement and instructional support. *Review of Educational Research*, *59*, 65–86.

ABOUT THE AUTHOR

Todd Stanley is the author of seven teacher education books including *Project-Based Learning for Gifted Students: A Handbook for the 21st-Century Classroom* and *Performance-Based Assessment for 21st-Century Skills*. He was a classroom teacher for 19 years, teaching students as young as second graders and as old as high school seniors, and was a National Board Certified teacher. He helped create a gifted academy for grades 5–8, which employs inquiry-based learning, project-based learning, and performance-based assessment. He is currently gifted services coordinator for Pickerington Local School District, OH, where he lives with his wife, Nicki, and two daughters, Anna and Abby.

COMMON CORE STATE STANDARDS ALIGNMENT

Projects	Grade Level	Common Core State Standards
Project 1	Grade 3	RL.3.1 Ask and answer questions to demonstrate understanding of a text, referring explicitly to the text as the basis for the answers.
		SL.3.4 Report on a topic or text, tell a story, or recount an experience with appropriate facts and relevant, descriptive details, speaking clearly at an understandable pace.
	Grade 4	RL.4.1 Refer to details and examples in a text when explaining what the text says explicitly and when drawing inferences from the text.
		SL.4.4 Report on a topic or text, tell a story, or recount an experience in an organized manner, using appropriate facts and relevant, descriptive details to support main ideas or themes; speak clearly at an understandable pace.
	Grade 5	RL.5.1 Quote accurately from a text when explaining what the text says explicitly and when drawing inferences from the text.
		SL.5.4 Report on a topic or text or present an opinion, sequencing ideas logically and using appropriate facts and relevant, descriptive details to support main ideas or themes; speak clearly at an understandable pace
Project 2	Grade 3	W.3.1 Write opinion pieces on topics or texts, supporting a point of view with reasons.
		SL.3.4 Report on a topic or text, tell a story, or recount an experience with appropriate facts and relevant, descriptive details, speaking clearly at an understandable pace.

Projects	Grade Level	Common Core State Standards
Project 2, *continued*	Grade 3, *continued*	SL.3.5 Create engaging audio recordings of stories or poems that demonstrate fluid reading at an understandable pace; add visual displays when appropriate to emphasize or enhance certain facts or details.
		SL.3.6 Speak in complete sentences when appropriate to task and situation in order to provide requested detail or clarification.
	Grade 4	W.4.1 Write opinion pieces on topics or texts, supporting a point of view with reasons and information.
		SL.4.4 Report on a topic or text, tell a story, or recount an experience in an organized manner, using appropriate facts and relevant, descriptive details to support main ideas or themes; speak clearly at an understandable pace.
		SL.4.5 Add audio recordings and visual displays to presentations when appropriate to enhance the development of main ideas or themes.
		SL.4.6 Differentiate between contexts that call for formal English (e.g., presenting ideas) and situations where informal discourse is appropriate (e.g., small-group discussion); use formal English when appropriate to task and situation.
	Grade 5	W.5.1 Write opinion pieces on topics or texts, supporting a point of view with reasons and information.
		SL.5.4 Report on a topic or text or present an opinion, sequencing ideas logically and using appropriate facts and relevant, descriptive details to support main ideas or themes; speak clearly at an understandable pace.
		SL.5.5 Include multimedia components (e.g., graphics, sound) and visual displays in presentations when appropriate to enhance the development of main ideas or themes.
		SL.5.6 Adapt speech to a variety of contexts and tasks, using formal English when appropriate to task and situation.
Project 3	Grade 3	W.3.3 Write narratives to develop real or imagined experiences or events using effective technique, descriptive details, and clear event sequences.
		SL.3.2 Determine the main ideas and supporting details of a text read aloud or information presented in diverse media and formats, including visually, quantitatively, and orally.
	Grade 4	W.4.3 Write narratives to develop real or imagined experiences or events using effective technique, descriptive details, and clear event sequences.

Projects	Grade Level	Common Core State Standards
Project 3, *continued*	Grade 4, *continued*	SL.4.2 Paraphrase portions of a text read aloud or information presented in diverse media and formats, including visually, quantitatively, and orally.
	Grade 5	W.5.3 Write narratives to develop real or imagined experiences or events using effective technique, descriptive details, and clear event sequences.
		SL.5.2 Summarize a written text read aloud or information presented in diverse media and formats, including visually, quantitatively, and orally.
Project 4	Grade 3	W.3.3 Write narratives to develop real or imagined experiences or events using effective technique, descriptive details, and clear event sequences.
		SL.3.2 Determine the main ideas and supporting details of a text read aloud or information presented in diverse media and formats, including visually, quantitatively, and orally.
	Grade 4	W.4.3 Write narratives to develop real or imagined experiences or events using effective technique, descriptive details, and clear event sequences.
		SL.4.2 Paraphrase portions of a text read aloud or information presented in diverse media and formats, including visually, quantitatively, and orally.
	Grade 5	W.5.3 Write narratives to develop real or imagined experiences or events using effective technique, descriptive details, and clear event sequences.
		SL.5.2 Summarize a written text read aloud or information presented in diverse media and formats, including visually, quantitatively, and orally.
Project 5	Grade 3	W.3.3 Write narratives to develop real or imagined experiences or events using effective technique, descriptive details, and clear event sequences.
		SL.3.2 Determine the main ideas and supporting details of a text read aloud or information presented in diverse media and formats, including visually, quantitatively, and orally.
	Grade 4	W.4.3 Write narratives to develop real or imagined experiences or events using effective technique, descriptive details, and clear event sequences.
		SL.4.2 Paraphrase portions of a text read aloud or information presented in diverse media and formats, including visually, quantitatively, and orally.

Projects	Grade Level	Common Core State Standards
Project 5, *continued*	Grade 5	W.5.3 Write narratives to develop real or imagined experiences or events using effective technique, descriptive details, and clear event sequences.
		SL.5.2 Summarize a written text read aloud or information presented in diverse media and formats, including visually, quantitatively, and orally.
Project 6	Grade 3	W.3.4 With guidance and support from adults, produce writing in which the development and organization are appropriate to task and purpose.
		W.3.6 With guidance and support from adults, use technology to produce and publish writing (using keyboarding skills) as well as to interact and collaborate with others.
		L.3.1 Demonstrate command of the conventions of standard English grammar and usage when writing or speaking.
		L.3.2 Demonstrate command of the conventions of standard English capitalization, punctuation, and spelling when writing.
	Grade 4	W.4.4 Produce clear and coherent writing in which the development and organization are appropriate to task, purpose, and audience.
		W.4.6 With some guidance and support from adults, use technology, including the Internet, to produce and publish writing as well as to interact and collaborate with others; demonstrate sufficient command of keyboarding skills to type a minimum of one page in a single sitting.
		L.4.1 Demonstrate command of the conventions of standard English grammar and usage when writing or speaking.
		L.4.2 Demonstrate command of the conventions of standard English capitalization, punctuation, and spelling when writing.
	Grade 5	W.5.4 Produce clear and coherent writing in which the development and organization are appropriate to task, purpose, and audience. (Grade-specific expectations for writing types are defined in standards 1–3 above.)
		W.5.6 With some guidance and support from adults, use technology, including the Internet, to produce and publish writing as well as to interact and collaborate with others; demonstrate sufficient command of keyboarding skills to type a minimum of two pages in a single sitting.
		L.5.1 Demonstrate command of the conventions of standard English grammar and usage when writing or speaking.

Projects	Grade Level	Common Core State Standards
Project 6, *continued*	Grade 5, *continued*	L.5.2 Demonstrate command of the conventions of standard English capitalization, punctuation, and spelling when writing.
Project 7	Grade 3	W.3.3 Write narratives to develop real or imagined experiences or events using effective technique, descriptive details, and clear event sequences.
		W.3.4 With guidance and support from adults, produce writing in which the development and organization are appropriate to task and purpose.
		W.3.5 With guidance and support from peers and adults, develop and strengthen writing as needed by planning, revising, and editing.
		L.3.3 Use knowledge of language and its conventions when writing, speaking, reading, or listening
	Grade 4	W.4.3 Write narratives to develop real or imagined experiences or events using effective technique, descriptive details, and clear event sequences.
		W.4.4 Produce clear and coherent writing in which the development and organization are appropriate to task, purpose, and audience.
		W.4.5 With guidance and support from peers and adults, develop and strengthen writing as needed by planning, revising, and editing.
		L.4.3 Use knowledge of language and its conventions when writing, speaking, reading, or listening.
	Grade 5	W.5.3 Write narratives to develop real or imagined experiences or events using effective technique, descriptive details, and clear event sequences.
		W.5.4 Produce clear and coherent writing in which the development and organization are appropriate to task, purpose, and audience.
		W.5.5 With guidance and support from peers and adults, develop and strengthen writing as needed by planning, revising, editing, rewriting, or trying a new approach.
		L.5.3 Use knowledge of language and its conventions when writing, speaking, reading, or listening.
		L.5.3a Expand, combine, and reduce sentences for meaning, reader/listener interest, and style.
Project 8	Grade 3	RI.3.2 Determine the main idea of a text; recount the key details and explain how they support the main idea.
		RI.3.6 Distinguish their own point of view from that of the author of a text.

Projects	Grade Level	Common Core State Standards
Project 8 *continued*	Grade 3, *continued*	RI.3.8 Describe the logical connection between particular sentences and paragraphs in a text (e.g., comparison, cause/effect, first/second/third in a sequence).
		W.3.1 Write opinion pieces on topics or texts, supporting a point of view with reasons.
		W.3.8 Recall information from experiences or gather information from print and digital sources; take brief notes on sources and sort evidence into provided categories.
	Grade 4	RI.4.2 Determine the main idea of a text and explain how it is supported by key details; summarize the text.
		RI.4.6 Compare and contrast a firsthand and secondhand account of the same event or topic; describe the differences in focus and the information provided..
		RI.4.8 Explain how an author uses reasons and evidence to support particular points in a text.
		W.4.1 Write opinion pieces on topics or texts, supporting a point of view with reasons and information.
		W.4.8 Recall relevant information from experiences or gather relevant information from print and digital sources; take notes and categorize information, and provide a list of sources.
		W.4.9 Draw evidence from literary or informational texts to support analysis, reflection, and research.
	Grade 5	RI.5.2 Determine two or more main ideas of a text and explain how they are supported by key details; summarize the text.
		RI.5.6 Analyze multiple accounts of the same event or topic, noting important similarities and differences in the point of view they represent.
		RI.5.8 Explain how an author uses reasons and evidence to support particular points in a text, identifying which reasons and evidence support which point(s).
		W.5.1 Write opinion pieces on topics or texts, supporting a point of view with reasons and information.
		W.5.8 Recall relevant information from experiences or gather relevant information from print and digital sources; summarize or paraphrase information in notes and finished work, and provide a list of sources.
		W.5.9 Draw evidence from literary or informational texts to support analysis, reflection, and research.
Project 9	Grade 3	RI.3.1 Ask and answer questions to demonstrate understanding of a text, referring explicitly to the text as the basis for the answers.

Projects	Grade Level	Common Core State Standards
Project 9, *continued*	Grade 3, *continued*	RI.3.7 Use information gained from illustrations (e.g., maps, photographs) and the words in a text to demonstrate understanding of the text (e.g., where, when, why, and how key events occur).
		RI.3.9 Compare and contrast the most important points and key details presented in two texts on the same topic.
		W.3.2 Write informative/explanatory texts to examine a topic and convey ideas and information clearly.
		W.3.7 Conduct short research projects that build knowledge about a topic.
		W.3.10 Write routinely over extended time frames (time for research, reflection, and revision) and shorter time frames (a single sitting or a day or two) for a range of discipline-specific tasks, purposes, and audiences.
	Grade 4	RI.4.1 Refer to details and examples in a text when explaining what the text says explicitly and when drawing inferences from the text.
		RI.4.7 Interpret information presented visually, orally, or quantitatively (e.g., in charts, graphs, diagrams, time lines, animations, or interactive elements on Web pages) and explain how the information contributes to an understanding of the text in which it appears.
		RI.4.9 Integrate information from two texts on the same topic in order to write or speak about the subject knowledgeably.
		W.4.2 Write informative/explanatory texts to examine a topic and convey ideas and information clearly.
		W.4.7 Conduct short research projects that build knowledge through investigation of different aspects of a topic.
		W.4.10 Write routinely over extended time frames (time for research, reflection, and revision) and shorter time frames (a single sitting or a day or two) for a range of discipline-specific tasks, purposes, and audiences.
	Grade 5	RI.5.1 Quote accurately from a text when explaining what the text says explicitly and when drawing inferences from the text.
		RI.5.7 Draw on information from multiple print or digital sources, demonstrating the ability to locate an answer to a question quickly or to solve a problem efficiently.
		RI.5.9 Integrate information from several texts on the same topic in order to write or speak about the subject knowledgeably.
		W.5.2 Write informative/explanatory texts to examine a topic and convey ideas and information clearly.

Projects	Grade Level	Common Core State Standards
Project 9, *continued*	Grade 5, *continued*	W.5.7 Conduct short research projects that use several sources to build knowledge through investigation of different aspects of a topic.
		W.5.10 Write routinely over extended time frames (time for research, reflection, and revision) and shorter time frames (a single sitting or a day or two) for a range of discipline-specific tasks, purposes, and audiences.
Project 10	Grade 3	RL.3.5 Refer to parts of stories, dramas, and poems when writing or speaking about a text, using terms such as chapter, scene, and stanza; describe how each successive part builds on earlier sections.
	Grade 4	RL.4.5 Explain major differences between poems, drama, and prose, and refer to the structural elements of poems (e.g., verse, rhythm, meter) and drama (e.g., casts of characters, settings, descriptions, dialogue, stage directions) when writing or speaking about a text.
	Grade 5	RL.5.5 Explain how a series of chapters, scenes, or stanzas fits together to provide the overall structure of a particular story, drama, or poem.
		RL.5.7 Analyze how visual and multimedia elements contribute to the meaning, tone, or beauty of a text (e.g., graphic novel, multimedia presentation of fiction, folktale, myth, poem).
		RI.5.7 Draw on information from multiple print or digital sources, demonstrating the ability to locate an answer to a question quickly or to solve a problem efficiently.
		RI.5.10 By the end of the year, read and comprehend informational texts, including history/social studies, science, and technical texts, at the high end of the grades 4–5 text complexity band independently and proficiently.